A RUMOURED CITY

A Rumoured City
NEW POETS FROM HULL

edited by Douglas Dunn

with a foreword by
Philip Larkin

BLOODAXE BOOKS

ISBN: 0 906427 41 X

First published 1982 by
Bloodaxe Books Ltd,
P.O. Box 1SN,
Newcastle upon Tyne NE99 1SN.

The publisher acknowledges the financial assistance
of Northern Arts.

Typesetting & cover printing by
Tyneside Free Press Workshop Ltd, Newcastle upon Tyne.

Printed in Great Britain by
Unwin Brothers Ltd, Old Woking, Surrey.

CONTENTS

MARGOT K. JUBY

SEAN O'BRIEN

TONY PETCH

FOREWORD

Poetry, like prose, happens anywhere. Hull got its clearance on this from Andrew Marvell many years ago; and if that singular Member of Parliament would have little in common with today's ancient and modern city lodged unexpectedly in the triangle of flat country between the Humber and the North Sea, it is still as good a place to write in as any.

Better, in fact, than some. For a place cannot produce poems: it can only not prevent them, and Hull is good at that. It neither impresses nor insists. When your train comes to rest in Paragon Station against a row of docile buffers, you alight with an end-of-the-line sense of freedom. Signs in foreign languages welcome you. Outside is a working city, yet one neither clenched in the blackened grip of the industrial revolution nor hiding behind a cathedral to pretend it is York or Canterbury. Unpretentious, recent, full of shops and special offers like a television commercial, it might be Australia or America, until you come upon Trinity House or the Dock Offices. For Hull has its own sudden elegancies.

People are slow to leave it, quick to return. And there are others who come, as they think, for a year or two, and stay a lifetime, sensing that they have found a city that is in the world, yet sufficiently on the edge of it to have a different resonance. Behind Hull is the plain of Holderness, lonelier and lonelier, and after that the birds and lights of Spurn Head, and then the sea. One can go ten years without seeing these things, yet they are always there, giving Hull the air of having its face half-turned towards distance and silence, and what lies beyond them.

These poems are not about Hull, yet it is unseen in all of them, the permission of a town that lets you write.

PHILIP LARKIN

ACKNOWLEDGEMENTS

Some of the poems in this anthology have appeared in the following publications: *Arvon Foundation Poetry Competition 1980 Anthology* (Kilnhurst, 1982), *Critical Quarterly, Encounter, The Gregory Awards 1980* (Secker & Warburg, 1981), *The Honest Ulsterman, London Magazine, New Poetry 6* (Hutchinson/Arts Council–P.E.N., 1980), *The New Review, Outcrop, Poetry Review, Poetry Supplement* (Poetry Book Society, Christmas 1979), *Proof, Quarto, Stone Ferry Review, The Times Literary Supplement, To Build a Bridge* (Lincolnshire & Humberside Arts Association, 1982), *Wave*, and *Yorkshire Review*. Some poems were broadcast on *Poetry Now* (BBC Radio 3) and by BBC Radio Humberside.

Seven poems by Peter Didsbury are taken from his collection *The Butchers of Hull* (Bloodaxe Books, 1982) and four by Tony Flynn from his book *A Strange Routine* (Bloodaxe Books, 1980). Sean O'Brien's book *The Indoor Park* (Bloodaxe Books, late 1982) includes all the poems of his selection.

INTRODUCTION

Like most cities built on the bank of an estuary, Hull has a marginal, provisional, almost frontier quality. It is a city of generous character, and it is difficult to live in it for any length of time and remain oblivious of its available but indefinable identity. Hull may be flat and lacking in landmarks or elegant streets—it is no Edinburgh, or Bath; it has never been fashionable or immodestly rich—but there is something in Hull which encourages an imaginative response to corners and details, sights and sounds, the effects of light and seasons.

Not only does Hull appeal to the imagination, but the longer you live here the more you become aware that it is a town which by its nature recommends the plainly human, the seriousness of what, in more glamorous places, is taken to be ordinary; it leads a writer to meditate on the rag and bone shop of the heart. Looked at from elsewhere, it may seem a backwater on the map of Britain. Lived in, though, and it is seen to have its own backwaters, to have its own map of lives and places, to be its own world.

Whether these impressions have registered on the writers included in this anthology of younger or under-published poets who have lived and worked in Hull is, perhaps, more speculative than certain. Hull's influence on them has been insidious rather than exact. Just by being here, they have experienced some of the imprecise phenomena that encourage poetry *via* Hull's present tense, by, for instance, evenings of eastern England perceived and wondered at in the soft urban dusks of summer, the strange light of autumn and winter, the days of spring in a city that has many trees.

Where writers work, over a period of time, is likely to contribute to how their words, forms and subjects are shaped. Other factors are involved: literary influence may be more important than topographical atmospherics. But I am not so sure if that is always the case. What is the larger conceiving force in a poet's imagination?—the phenomena of nature, and character, working against the background of a place, or a style of writing arranged from reading and original gifts? One can hardly exist without the other, no matter which part of the question you put first.

Certainly, an important if hardly tangible ingredient in some of the poems which follow this essay, were the talking-

shops in which they were discussed, as well as literary compan-
ionship in general. Although present at only some of these
conversations, it is difficult for me to be other than subjective
in describing a local literary curiosity—a coincidence of talents
and atmosphere at one moment of time, one which detracts
nothing from the individuals involved.

Many poets are approached by writers younger than them,
or other aspirants, in the hope of hearing revelatory criticism,
or even the secrets of verse. Neither expectation is ever
satisfied, I suspect, although there is no harm in trying.
Unsuited by inclination or temperament to behave like
Svengali, my own mind was changed in these critical sessions
as often as my original point of view was accepted. Sulks,
silences, loggerheads, insults, manic arias, surprise, delight,
approval, disapproval—these are among the characteristics of
the candid literary talking-shop. I don't mean—or I don't
mean it necessarily—that when I have seen the work of many
of the poets in this anthology, they have refused to take a
telling. Given advice, though, some have been known to imply
(and some have been known to shout), 'When I want your
advice, I'll ask for it.'

Between 1974 and 1975, when I was seeing regularly poems
by Tony Flynn, Ian Gregson and Tony Griffin, I was impressed
by how they discussed the formidable problems of contemp-
orary poetic style. Flynn's intelligence was schooled in
philosophy and theology, and is as forceful as his obvious
principle, which is to write poems grounded on actuality and
experience. He writes frequently through attitudes to his
working-class Catholic background although his sense of the
values of art is always present. Reared on English and American
literature, Gregson's intelligence, I noticed, responded
differently to the questions we discussed. At times I felt myself
to be a privileged observer of two lively minds coming to terms
with a fluid and transitional moment of poetry. Yet if their
responses were different from each other, it was obvious that
their poems had concerns in common—Gregson's poetry is as
personal as Flynn's, equally interested in narratives drawn
from experience and turned into the fictions of life, while
Gregson, too, draws on his background, childhood and family.
Griffin's poetry, more mystical and visionary than Flynn's or
Gregson's, added an interesting dimension to the debate. How

far can poetry, or the imagination, go on faith, on untested assumptions of the poet's value, without losing sight of its terrestrial, quotidian beginnings? These were sometimes heady conversations, of great personal value to me, whatever they might have meant to the other participants. They argued with the fervour of men in their mid-20s, a passion, which, if I have yet to outlive it, I was then beginning to observe in myself with the increasingly ironic habits of maturity. Since then, their work has found favour with editors and publishers. At that time, though, they were publishing little or nothing at all. They were scanning the prints with the fury and contempt of tyros, reading and talking with an enthusiasm which, at their age, I had never known, for the simple reason that if others were writing they kept it pretty exclusive, or secret.

Margot Juby and Genny Rahtz were also students at the University of Hull in 1974-75, and I first saw their poems then, although I saw little of them immediately afterwards. Margot Juby's work is aggressively feminist. She also describes herself as a nihilist. Her influences range from Marvell and the Brothers Grimm to R.D. Laing and The Velvet Underground, a far cry from the British and American poetry that have been valuable to Flynn and Gregson, Peter Didsbury, Tony Petch, Douglas Houston and Sean O'Brien.

Hull is gently if consistently present in Genny Rahtz's poems. One of them is named for the city—'this subdued city,' she calls it, 'Providing for its livelihood/Not its looks . . .' "Abstract" is a word she uses more than once, suggesting that modern painting is as important to her as poetry. 'Ashtray' and 'Id Mud' seem written with a painterly eye, while the latter poem reminds me of the estuarial paintings of John Pettenuzzo, an artist who lives and works in Hull.

Frank Redpath is older than the other contributors, and different from them in that his poems show distinctly Larkin-esque habits of expression. Larkin's presence in Hull might be expected to have registered more in terms of influence. As it is, his mark is indelible in terms of admiration. Wry, neat, always nicely concluded, Redpath's poems interested me first when I read a few in *Wave*, a poetry magazine edited and printed by Ted Tarling in Hull between 1970 and 1974. 'To the Village' captures perfectly these out-of-the-way villages of Holderness and the East Riding, or the northern part of

Lincolnshire. 'In and Out' evokes November in the moody long gardens of Hull's Avenues district.

It has to be stated in plain and simple English that my contributors detest the prospect of being labelled "provincial". It is a danger which a book of this kind courts, in a literary climate which specializes in those pejorative ciphers which seem to breed like bacteria on the tip of the English critical tongue. Margot Juby's dismissals of sexual humbug, the extremes to which she is prepared to take her provocations and accusations, is only one case in point. Reader, they are probably less provincial than you are, even if they live, or have lived, in a city which has a fondness for the parochial and an unenviably jocular reputation for being provincial, that is, outside its boundaries.

Born in Cardiff, spending much of his schooldays in Scotland, Douglas Houston writes with an engaging gift for rhetoric of a sort which elevates literary panache above perceptions of place. 'Cemetery' is about October's effect on the old burial ground on Hull's Spring Bank West, while 'Driver' embodies the estuarial feeling by which several of the poets who have written in Hull have been tantalized. 'The Others', and 'Devotions', witty and inventive, are more characteristic of Houston, a poet who tries to balance the erudite with the colloquial, urbane with vernacular sentiments. His poems are unashamedly literary, a trait he has in common with Sean O'Brien. Yet Houston was not always that sort of poet. Years ago, when we were undergraduates together in Hull, I remember being baffled by his occasional psychedelic rhapsodies. They were all the more bewildering for being interspersed with concise imagistic poems.

Now in his mid-30s, Peter Didsbury has for years dedicated himself to expressing the often strange patterns of imagery and statement which his imagination produces. It is pleasing to know that his book *The Butchers of Hull* has now been published by Bloodaxe, for I had begun to feel that Didsbury's poetry was of the sort which insular British taste might consign to little magazines and to nowhere else. His work looks at first sight as if it is "difficult", but in fact it's not. Frequently, the act of imagining appears to be laid bare in Didsbury's poems as much as the objects which his imagination serves. His learning draws from all sorts of sources, ancient and modern, but it is always sentient. There is nothing provincial about his work, either: it aligns itself with the poetry of John Ashbery and Christopher Middleton.

Didsbury avoids metre and rhyme, as if he has successfully escaped from traditional forms. Sean O'Brien, however, while he admires Didsbury's work as much as I do, entertains the possibility of an up-dated traditional elegance. Sometimes obsessively trisyllabic, his lines tilt against his rhythms with a fierce "I-won't-take-No-for-an-answer" kind of stylishness. In O'Brien's work, the educated idioms of contemporary verse are sieved through a nervy, critical experience of contemporary life. His curious blend of direct and unexpected images and statements is a technique he has in common with Didsbury. 'The Lamp', for instance, performs a wonderful transformation on the Anglepoise lamp which the poem contemplates, and, as Anglepoise lamps have been around in poems rather a lot these days I should, for O'Brien's sake, point out that his poem has existed for several years. 'Walking' and 'The Snowfield' both mention 'the planthouse' in Pearson Park to which O'Brien's imagination has returned more than twice. But Hull slides into his poems unbidden, as it does in Houston's or Didsbury's: it amounts to an unforced seizure of images which are to hand and which have been lived through by more than the eye. Sean O'Brien's first book *The Indoor Park* is to be published by Bloodaxe later this year.

Stone Ferry Review, which O'Brien founded and edited in 1978, was a periodical I felt might express the way poetry was discussed and valued in Hull by its editor and his friends and supporters. Possessed of a critically fertile mind and a short way with fools, O'Brien proved to have all the editorial gifts except endurance: the magazine folded after two issues. In a way, though, it proved a stimulus, in spite of its brief existence. A magazine can give contributors close to it a sudden focus, something to care for, and I noticed that the poetry of Douglas Houston, Peter Didsbury and Tony Petch began to improve by leaps and bounds as if, like O'Brien, they sensed that they were about to enter a larger literary arena than Hull itself had to offer.

Among those that *Stone Ferry Review* printed, Tony Petch, a relative newcomer to Hull, was certainly leaving behind the inelegant poetry of his earlier days. Petch has shown a lack of patience with much of contemporary British poetry and feels his debts are owed to Ashbery, Kenneth Koch and Eastern European poetry in translation. Yet I find something incorrigibly English about his nature imagery in 'The Owl' or 'Mushrooming' and in the entire cast of 'Cider-making in Herefordshire'. It is close to the kind of Englishness I sense in Didsbury's 'The Drainage', where he imagines Hull back into its state of nature, or 'In Britain'. That is, it is deep, and imaginative.

Comparing Petch's style with Douglas Houston's, with Flynn's, Gregson's, or any other of these poets, is to notice a contrast in literary values. They may all be gathered between the same covers, as if under the same banner, but the flag is the flag of poetry—the Jolly Roger with crossed bottles—and not of a coterie sharing the same assumptions. They are clearly different from each other, and yet Hull has at some time in their writing lives acted on them as a catalyst, as a "place of writing". There have been good times in that place, days and nights to remember.

DOUGLAS DUNN

PETER DIDSBURY

The Nail

I'm knocking a nail in.
With my heart.
The darts are on silent running.
Then they thud home.
The players call to each other.
Or rock on tables.
The music's too loud.
It involves the lungs with the sternum.
The blue-lipped male stuffs food down his throat.
I regard his opposable thumbs.
Beer left standing ebbs and flows with the moon.
There are arcane tides.
Still chambers in the hearts of gorillas
Fill with phlegm and clutter.
Gentle families cough and die on gravel-shelves.
They rinse small bitter plums.
Or else are here in this bass thump.
There are worlds of call and colour.
A stretched clock in the breast.
I'm knocking a sandwich home.
I'm knocking a nail in.
I'm hammering with my blood.

The Specialist Heart

My inside pocket is my specialist heart.
I feeds it with papers.
We have filed our jackets with regularity
my fathers and I,
we make wardrobes into libraries.
Letterheads bills and annotated bootlace-papers
are our bones and our memories:
we write in indelible.
Our pockets swell to the old afflatus
of a war against women:

hushed tones, and angry glances.
Once a year, on Mischief Night
we frighten ourselves on the old stories
of female victories: jackets gone to jumble
and vanished patrimonies.
The pocketsful which made us stoop
to beauty or degradations
lie bundled by marriages.
My dads and I put in and in
for rust and moth
to work into treasuries.
The paper folds and un-folds
to make the cross that eats the paper.
We do a lot of unfolding, then.
We have learned to put in and in
to have our histories,
to build archivists' hearts.
It becomes a racial tradition
in the recent generations.
The discipline has settled
into generous options.
We know when to kill ourselves now,
how not to end up stinking of tobacco.

Two Urns

> *"Tis time to observe Occurrences, and let nothing
> remarkable escape us'* – Sir Thomas Browne

Long expected they arrive at last,
maybe from the coast of Africa,
two urns that now stand breathing quietly
beneath the wall of the shed,
between the keg of earth and the water butt,
like patient animals. They come at night.
I go to my back window and can just make out
their grey flanks like elephant hide
heave down twice into a stiff slow pulse,
cooling and beginning to reserve
the silver air of this specific garden.

Algeria burned, or Tunis impelled them
to come where the soft fruit-canes
would stand on the wind in salutation,
tulip and big daisy and phlox
calling to my migratory jars
to crumble into sand and reconstitute here,
where I welcome them. They stand in air
and the grass grows up around their feet
and rain collects and dries inside them.
By day they swell until they speak like drums
and at midnight I can bend my ear to them
or watch from the doorway the stars to which they call,
pulling their hard coats closer about them,
swallowing white fire,
working their round mouths on Sun and Moon
or the flight of birds, woodsmoke, silence,
the tracks of this or that slow planet.

The Drainage

When he got out of bed the world had changed.
It was very cold. His breath whitened the room.
Chill December clanked at the panes.
There was freezing fog.
He stepped outside.
Not into his street but a flat wet landscape.
Sluices. Ditches. Drains. Frozen mud and leafcake. Dykes.
He found he knew the names of them all.
Barber's Cut. Cold Track. Lament. Meridian Stream.
He found himself walking.
It was broad cold day but the sky was black.
Instead of the sun it was Orion there.
Seeming to pulse his meaning down.
He was naked. He had to clothe himself.
The heifers stood like statues in the fields.
They didn't moan when he sliced the hides from them.
He looked at the penknife in his hand.
The needle, the thread, the clammy strips.
Now his face mooned out through a white hole.

The cape dripped. He knew he had
the bounds of a large parish to go.
His feet refused to falter.
Birds sat still in the trees.
Fast with cold glue. Passing their clumps
he watched them rise in their species.
The individuals. Sparrow. Starling. Wren.
He brought them down with his finger.
Knife needle and thread again.
It happened with the streams.
Pike barbel roach minnow gudgeon.
Perch dace eel. Grayling lamprey bream.
His feet cracked puddles and were cut on mud. They bled.
There was movement. He pointed. He stitched.
His coat hung reeking on him.
He made cut after cut in the cold.
Coldness and the colours of blood.
Red blue and green. He glistened.
He stitched through white fat.
Weight of pelts and heads. Nodding at the hem.
Feathers. Scales. Beaks and strips of skin.
He had the bounds of a large parish to go.
Oh Christ, he moaned. Sweet Christ.
The Hunter hung stretched in the Sky.
He looked at the creatures of the bankside.
He glistened. He pointed. He stitched.

Home Town

Children and dead sailors lounge in salty parks
or lie parcelled in oilskins in boarded-up shops.
He strolls among them with a sword
or finds himself alone by a grey and angry sea.
There is much to terrify in this seaside town.
A striding man from a medicine show
treads on the middle air and scowls at him.
A wind machine blows scraps of alphabets
which burn about his ears. He steps into an upper room
and the floor is no floor, but an idle bed of dangerous machinery.

He could have perished in those engines,
or fallen right through the house.
How does he always rescue himself? He does not.
Surely one of these escapades would suffice to encompass his
death?
It would, but something always rescues him.
Dark children offer him their hands in parks
that bob against the street like barges against a wharf.
The drowned recline on their elbows
and smile at a bureaucratic mistake.
Perilous climbs bring him out of the theatre
and the wheels that should have burst him open
never get further than starting to turn.
What is beginning to frighten him most is the rescue,
not the predicament. If the charred ideograms would turn to
rain
he could believe in it, but they simply cease to blow.
The vaudeville morgues are not consumed in a flame,
he just leaves them behind him on a drizzling quay.
The hand that pulls him from the cogs and gears
is not attached to an Angel but only to the dark in the doorway.
He parks his ancient Austin Seven on a steeply shelving beach
and leaves the handbrake off, for it will not plunge
into the tall unconscious waters but simply wait,
between the ocean and the town. He crunches shingle,
and wags his sword at the flapping bones of a winter resort.
His car stands patiently, with her head between her wheels.

The Northlands

No rain. No storm or thunder,
not even on the wireless. No lightning,
no rain.

But I'd been watching the lightning!
Either bounced off local cloud
or reflected in lucid mesmeric radio
from over the horizon

three whole days now,
which nobody else had,
and for three whole days I'd
thought I had epilepsy.

Not until I heard some tune
I hadn't been listening to
and which didn't impress me
was a Chopin nocturne
and saw how it and the night sustained each other
like two old con men telling each other tales
did I actually get the point,
and the intimate cruelty,
of the day's imitations:

a casual spread of laundry in the bath—Ophelia;
creased and mottled leaves from Summer
on Susan's Miss Moffat cap—the cunning Butterfly;
myself with fountain pen in hand,
—ah how much better than history.

Which is why
I'm confessing from here it was from here the first time round
that the lies *really* began and I began to imagine
the hills with all their electrics stilled
and *cattle pinned out like photofits in the glare*
and *my house that laughed in a curtain of rain*
but didn't embarrass me, though it should have done,
and even . . . .
if I'd died that night how it wouldn't have meant
quitting this kingdom of metaphor
but leaping off the body fag in hand
to be some new kind of god for the northlands,
the *northlands*,
which actually frighten me,
which far from being a place
are a set of sounds whose transcription I think
it would be unwise to leave unrepented for very long,
whose transcription thank God
I think I am *unable*
to leave unrepented very long.

Night Moves

'Workin' on mysteries, without any clues' – Bob Seger

He got much younger and smaller.
Two police arrived and took him out of the bar.
The street received him as a child.
He broke away when he spied the fortunate bus.
I had to throw a handful of coins to him.
Shillings and dirhems clanged on the metal floor.
Our policemen frighten me a lot.
They weren't in any hurry anyway,
standing by the railings in the dark.
They still had hold of his friend.
Their car was parked in the side road
that leads to the Royal Infirmary.
The yellow doorway crawled along the kerb,
the kid in a jersey, the conductor with a moustache.
I stayed crouching for a long time
as if on a sunlit bowling green.
My open hand was filling with sodium glow.
The gaze of the police was like
the nearness of the pavement to my knees.
Night's inexplicable actions. These night moves.
The railings released the breath they'd been
holding on to all day.

In Britain

The music, on fat bellied instruments.
The fingers, swarming down ladders
into the bubbling cauldrons of sound.
The mouths, greasy, encouraging the prying fingers
with songs of fecund stomachs.
The hands, transferring to the singing mouths
whatever is lifted through the scum.
The choicest morsels, the collops of dog and the
gobbets of pig. The orchestras and bands,

the minstrelsy arranged in tiers,
dripping on each other. The larded steps.
The treacherous floors in the wooden galleries.
The garlands of offal, plopping on heads
from a height of some feet.
The offal sliding off down the front of the face,
or over the neck and ears. The offal reposing like hats.
The curly grey-white tubes, dangling jauntily
above the left eye of the bagpipe player.
The guests, similarly festooned.
The guests at their conversation,
abundance of dogs and pigs in these islands.
The guests at their serious business, lying in pools.
The stories, farting and belching across the puddled boards.
The gross imaginations, bulging with viscera.
The heads full of stories, the stories thwacked like bladders.
The stories steaming in time to the music.
The stories, chewed like lumps of gristle.
The stories describing extravagant herds.
The stories, reasons for killing each other.

The Bell

The Europe of the heart,
and a bright wood there.
Listen to the bell.
The ears attend
the spasms of a yellow bell.
Breath from its old mouth
subdues the quilt of countries,
a blanket on a sickbed.
The squares of mustard and the squares of potato
crumple under the heat,
which ruts like dogs
on the uninspected roads.
The hot wall of twelve o'clock
pushes history west.
Barns go down. Fields and churches fall.
The land permits

a hard tide of trees.
It is eaten by roots.
The heel of a gnarled hand
forges and bakes,
ferments and brews.
Ponderous and momentary hands
have twisted rope in rope-walks
and cast a bell in sand.
Someone was lost once.
Someone still stands immured
inside cold masonry,
exercising sound.
In the Europe of the heart,
in a bright wood there,
The yellow is like the flat of a blade.
The heat is from a chill belfry,
moving west with the trees.

A Winter's Fancy

> *To write a TRISTRAM SHANDY or a SENTIMENTAL
> JOURNEY there is no way but to be Sterne; and Sternes
> are not turned out in bakers' batches.*

A winter's fancy.
I look out of my window
and perceive I am Laurence Sterne.
I am sitting in Shandy Hall.
It is raining.
I am inventing a Bag,
which will accommodate everything.
I'd weave it out of air if I could
but the rain slants down like a page of Greek
and the afternoon is a dish of mud,
far removed from gentle opinion.
I am heavy with God.
The weather used
to cloak itself in sentiment
but today it imitates the tongues of men
and wags in curtains at me, along a yard.

I am also John, an elderly bibliophile.
Once, long after I died, I returned to Coxwold
on a literary pilgrimage.
A red-faced lout leaned over my gate
and instructed me curtly to Sodding Sod Off.
He was full of choler.
I sometimes feel I can understand
what's been eluding me ever since Christmas.
I'm exhausting my karma of country parson
in a dozen lives of wit and kidneys,
caritas, the pox, and marbled endpapers.
Looking out from here, this afternoon,
I can just discern the porch of my church
where Nick and Numps are sheltering from
Thucydides, Books Six and Seven.
By the look of that cloud looming up like a skull
there will soon be nothing left to do
but to take to my bed.
The cattle squelch past beneath a sodden sky,
below my windows and before the eyes
of Peter Didsbury, in his 35th year.
I consider other inventions of mine,
which rise before me in the darkening pane.
Light me that candle, oh my clever hand,
for it is late, and I am admirably tired.

Back of the House

Sick of England, but happy in your garden
this hot afternoon, your English garden,
where everything looks like something else
and Language, fat and prone beneath her fountain,
idly dispenses curling parchment notes,
her coveted, worthless, licences to imitate.
There is too much to photograph here,
so put your camera down. Relax.
A fan of green depends from twigs like vines
but the punkah wallah has gone to stand
in the shade, where you cannot pick him out,

and grins at the print he left behind,
which moves its arm in air, and grins at *him*.
So pull the rope on the broken swing, to make us cool.
Impersonate a dancer from Bali or Siam,
or somewhere they posture with sticks and bits of string.
Look around you. That large bird was running away
from a poem by Keats, and it failed.
A pile of brushwood makes flagrant promises
to Andrew Marvell, and the boulevards are ringed by bombs.
Light, and shade, are the lustrations of *trompe l'oeil*,
itself the name of a garden in France,
and the three bleached poles that limit the brassica
make a hitching rail for goblin cavalry
in the childhood garden that continued to grow,
commensurate with our stature. 'How far we used
to travel in only three paces,' you say
as we take an unhurried dozen to the gate.
When I walk off down the hot brick lane
I know I leave myself behind
in the coloured window, in the Byzantine
back of the house. I watch us still examining
the blasted elm, that rocks to your fingers
and threatens to fall. It would lie across
half the garden. I estimate its height
and step that far away, before I go.

The Experts

A man who knows everything about pigeons
is talking to a man who thinks he's a Roman.
They are fishing the waters of the Kennet,
a stream that rises in the Marlborough Downs.
Their spinners with three hooks are meant for large perch
but what they come up with is chunky tesserae,
the ruined remains of an inundated pavement.
Few are the pleasures that can compare
with those afforded by a Berkshire July.
Everything has a Latin name
or speaks with the hollow mouth of history,

sits in a stand of trees and calls to you
or drags you under ground and breaks your bones.
At the next peg downstream their hirsute neighbour
has left his rod in its rest and is having lunch.
Holly-leaves in lard in a rich bronze pan
punctuate the noontide with their distinctive crackle
and a rainbow left by the recent showers
bends into the woods on the opposite bank.
It was hereabouts that a blacksmith once heard
a prolonged and derisive burst of cheering
that kept him sober ever afterwards,
at home with his wife and more careful of
his forge and the custom of his native shire.
'In Gervase Markham's *Farewell to Husbandry*,'
runs the cheerful banter along the bank,
'there are ox-shoes with fullered grooves and calkins,
and drag rakes and heel rakes with split willow handles.'
They take their meridian ease, these labouring men,
as experts in the field have always done.
Lying on their elbows and beneath the open sky
they ponder the stolen grass, the common stream,
break bread and cheese and eat their eccentric meats,
and as the thirsty ground dries out again
flex their muscles a bit, fall to bickering,
throw chips of twig and ancient dung around,
then belch, fall silent, and finally fall asleep.

Mappa Mundi
(for Alan Livingstone)

In their great houses there were always tables laid,
piled high with simple food and books,
old tables that lay supportive beneath
a drift of nutshells and paper, sharp tools.
Returned from walking behind the byre,
or spreading lant from casks upon the fields,
it was at these boards that they received
the urgent message from the capital,
pushing cheese and almanacks aside

to unroll the hasty map, slopping a harsh red wine
into bowls, spilling it, augmenting the stains.
Later, brooding idly and alone
upon required action they might scan
the worn incisements of their tutored days,
the musical notes whose deep square holes
enlaced a fertile cartography,
in which each emblematic creature rose
above a smoking town, and called aloud
to the beasts at the corners of the world.
It was cold, and there was all of Europe
to decide, and Europe, hooded like a bird,
blinked in its eye-gapes and shifted on its perch.
It was ice. The ink in its beechwood wells
snapped to the black attention of winter,
while fields lay supine in communion clothes
waiting for the word, and a coney limped
to the doorstep of the hall for warmth,
or just to perish there. Tables, shifted nearer
to the blaze, supported the elbows of men
who watched themselves in dreams, in the gases
vapours and *language* of the hearth, for they
etymologised, and watched for others too.
Logs of poplar's yellow wood, the splintered larch,
fed a conflagration which all men scanned
to know their mind or find their visitors:
still many hours away, for example, a grandee in furs
alights from his carriage at a crossroad in the hills
and knows he is regarded, as he bends
to fill the carcass of a fowl with snow,
as well as who regards him. His clear gaze
is lifted for a moment towards a house
he travels to but cannot see, then falls,
as the eyes of his host have also fallen,
back from this fire to an erudite table,
a table spread with the things of the world
and cut out from the local forest years ago.

TONY FLYNN

Jessica Drew's Married Son

Where streetlamps burn
their orange glare
through windows into rooms –
into a room;

by the bed a tattered
Roman missal, above it a bleeding Sacred Heart;

and Jessica Drew, five-days-dead,
is staring from her cold grey sheets
over dark roofs
and rain-drenched fields,

through centrally heated
air and through
his wife's blue chiffon evening-dress,

down the long curve
of his sleeping spine.

Father Michael's Waking Dream

She calls to him now
from the edge of the pool,

Bless me,
Father, for I have
sinned . . . .

Laughing
she steps
from her thin
blue dress,

. . . sticky
red leaves
in her matted hair, O
my sweet, my
precious one . . .

and turns from the trees
towards him.
                    His vision
swims and blurs.

He blinks –

The black dog sprawled
across her shadow, nosing her grassy
cleft, might be his cassock
sloughed on the lawn,

or his own shadow
darker on hers.

Veterans

We planned in cellars
at the burnt-out
heart of our city –

conspirators, the threatened
who fought from sewers
and bombed factories;

from a gutted church
where sudden flares
blazed through Gothic

windows, and shattered saints
scarred our knees
as we crawled to shadow

like rats—our teeth
at every booted
heel. Now

we are
free, and our teeth
rot. The enemy

has gone to ground –
whisperings behind
cold smiles and

reassuring nods, under pillows
at midnight, from the open mouths
of our sleeping wives.

The Servant's Tale

I rise, and am invisible
about the place . . . From the moment
I first kneel

at the cold hearth
with wood to set the fire there,
I am his servile

ghost of the rooms.
My name he neither knew
nor knows. But once he came late

to my attic-room; stumbled drunk
to my narrow bed . . . And I
complied—Not a word of command

from him but I lay
obedient beneath him there.
So easily did I attend,

I might have been pouring
his favourite wine. On his leaving I smoothed
the crumpled sheets

as if I were
clearing his place after dinner –
Day after day

and all through the house,
my snowfield, my linen field,
trampled and fouled.

A Mother's Death

Night, and your frail
plants exhaust our air.
                        In the washing-basket
soiled clothes accumulate.
Soon they will spill
into the room
and life will begin again –
they will wash their own socks.

These Hours

You will remember
none of this—these hours

in my arms, cradling
your fevered head against

my shirt—your small skull's
watermark impressed above my heart –

this room, the lullaby I sing
to your troubled dreams.

En Famille

With my head shaved and my face
painted blue, my nipples pierced and ear-rings
through, I'm ready to start the show.
The curtain rises. Birdsong and the blinding light.
Downstairs, in the wings,
my two small sons and their father rehearse
our dénouement, their sub-plot, my fall.

Night Song

The moon like a nun's
old face at the window,

your crumpled white dress
like a cloud on the chair . . .

And streetlamps burn
into our eyes.

So breathe in the candlesmoke,
catpiss, and rain;

lay my head on your belly
and pull up the sheet; bury us both

at the back of beyond,
where a slow stream

might wash away
bloodstains and brickdust

from hands
and hair,

ashes
from our burnt-out hearts.

After Mass

Sweet candle-smoke wreathed
the Virgin's

blue smile, and incense
sickened the air.

Behind the old mill? Theresa hissed,
as we dipped our fingers together into

the cold stone font
and blessed ourselves.

Girl on a Swing, 10.00pm

A cold wind streamed her hair,
unravelling the braid she wears for school;

and her forehead shone
in the distant glow from the motorway.

A deserted park, an empty swing,
and I remember how
as she walked past me towards the gates
I caught sight of her small school badge:

a heart, a wreath of thorns, Latin
circling her breast.

Wrong Address

I opened the door to a beaming priest
who said that a neighbour had phoned.
He was certain he'd got the right address
but not so sure of the dying man's name.
'Father, there's no one even ill,' I said,

and almost felt sorry to disappoint.
He braced himself and stood his ground, not
one to be rattled by facts: 'I'm convinced
it was Mr O'Regan . . . or was it
Mr Devine?' Confused, his heavy head
rolled back, and the stiff white collar
cut into his neck—he was squinting
through gold-rimmed specs at the sky, as if
elusive names appeared
above the roofs across the street.

                              He mused
a moment longer,
stroking his smooth
fat chin, before he finally had to admit
that perhaps it might be *Road* he wanted,
and not, as he thought, *Street.*

He thanked me politely and then walked back
to his Anglia parked at the gate.

                              And still
he hadn't remembered the name
of the man I imagined rehearsing
all of the sins that he'd saved till now
which had he confessed with the *little 'uns*
each month in the gloomy box
might have brought down on his happy life
this old priest's wily wrath: smiling disdain
at church bazaars, the knowing frown at Mass.

Last Rites

In nomine Patris, et Filii . . .

His hands flutter in the air above her –
candlelight trembles weak birds on the wall.

Her bony fingers clasp
a silver crucifix against
her breast.

When her thin
tongue flicks
across her lips, he thinks how like
a lizard she looks
pinned by some cruel child to this cold sheet.

In the next room
the old woman's son kneels by his bed
pleading with her favourite dress.

The Dandy's Dream

'*. . . to live and die before a mirror . . .*' – Baudelaire

How I love all
these mirrors, this glass!
To die like this would be

perfection—the blade held
to my throat, wide eyes
following its slow

descent, careful not to graze
or scar; and then
the breathless

pause
above my cock, dreaming
its soft fall

against my thigh.
Perfection: to fix
the grimace in my dying eyes,

and then to leave
this room, my body,
and the glass voyeur.

Les Poètes Maudits

After cutting a dashing figure
in the capital, seducing women
from every level of society –
rumours even of a Royal conquest –
I shall ruin myself at cards,
drink my health to its ebb,
retire to the country—a small
run-down estate—and die,
leaving my beautiful daughter penniless,

at the mercy of a writer who
invents a chance affair, sudden
marriage to a banker's son; children;
all that she desires; and for me
a grave she'll visit every Spring
with violets: forgiven, remembered only
for presents on birthdays,
surprises at Christmas, what I
might have been but for the world.

Lying Low

I am keeping notebooks, journals,
in a perfect
longhand, a scrupulous
calligraphy, copperplate on vellum.

Rapid, on-the-spot jottings
precede the final
painstaking entries.

No corrections or erasions mar
my cursive script—mistakes dictate
that I begin again.

Today I have
numbered the bones
of a small, dead bird;
plucked and counted every feather;
I have identified
each particle of food
that remained in its crop after death.

And when the sky flames
above the capital, my night is speaking
names in the dark, christening
specimens pressed
under glass,
        Carex montana . . .
vulpina . . . nigra . . .

—Keeping my head down,
lying low.

Boats for Hire

Drifting through fallen
floating leaves, trailing its oars

like two broken wings, our rowing boat
nudged the muddy bank, startling a swan and his mate.

We watched them rise,
followed their climb away from us,

and wished for them
a quiet lake, where only

their own reflections glide
between them on the water.

And you cannot pay
to row across it.

Since You Left

It is late and the house
is quiet . . . Late, and I am alone
in the room where I worked.
Behind the curtain are windows
like row upon row of open graves.
And there are dead stars there that shine
more brightly than the risen moon.
Your young face, framed
by a cold white sky, smiles down from the wall
above my desk. You are aboard
ship, ready to sail, and the decks are packed
with waving strangers who've watched me grow old.

Saint Francis

Crumbs of soil smudge
fingertips that lift
the small egg from its nest.

Cupped in his calloused
palm and held
perfectly still

to his ear,
he listens
and can hear,

through grey-green
speckled shell,
the dreaming white.

IAN GREGSON

Untune that String

The Castle Museum at York
has a reconstructed town,
Edwardian, all facade:
a grocer's, a confectioner's,
a post office, pharmacy
and shoe-shop, 'everything' (she said,
whom only the fire station excited)
that would allow them
to be better tied down.
She frowned, waist-deep in children
on a trip from school,
then caught in a couple's linked hands.
They had spent four nights together –
intricate knots and no strings.
He had begun to feel more
at home in her dressing-gown
when they stepped into this homeliness
anachronistic and complete.
Envying it he examined every shop.
Waxing sentimental about Lipton's
he listened to her turning flames on the town:
the drawing-room piano on fire,
homes broken, and all family ties.

Sam and Janet Evening

The crooner of American romance,
those lies; then me: 'There was this bloke . . .'
'My wife's so fat . . .' and this was us –
our marriage, real. No joke.

I slip deep into the hollow
worn in our bed and six men sag
under a coffin to the bar.
My straight face falls, I search for the tag.

I can't distinguish her from my lines;
twelve tables weep into their beer.
A life together: tag and punch.
Waking the dream starts—her fur
and her dresses dance from the wardrobe,
thin air impersonating her!

A Dental Appointment

The old kitchen, just before:
her arms heaped with washing, mouth gagged with pegs.
The walls sloughed and grew two skins,
cupboards fattened, smelling of paint,
the table lengthened and shone.

I'd hurried home, was missing my appointment,
while she was lying on the couch.
Twelve neighbours were pronouncing,
superstitiously, upon the danger,
when combined, of washing-day and dentistry.

My jagged tooth had done it.
Her right side was softening
into a mist I parted: the arm
was deadened, and the leg callipered.
And all the peggies on the carpet!

The couch was growing into the suite
it would be after she returned.
Her mouth fell open: all her conversations
chattered out high-pitched, rewinding;
her sentences were scrambled afterwards.

Ambulance men removed the old furniture,
the pegs were broken on the stone floor.
My tongue tested the half-gap of the snag,
my roots aching over older incisors;
removal men stretchered her away.

Crab Lane Village from the New Flats

The flat window can contain Crab Lane and more:
its blackened church, its cobbled hill that climbs
to a growing council estate. I see from here
how its boundaries, bounded by the window,
are lost in Manchester. I try to see
why anecdotes will not contain its past:
the punch-drunk boxer muttering
and shadow-punching through the streets;
the leader of the Whitsuntide procession,
retarded, strutting in army boots and bowler;
my grandfather, who dropped a ladder on his toe,
tied a slipper to his foot, and walked to work –
five miles in the snow. Those characters are caught
between before and after as by photographs,
survive in neither. They withdraw to where they live,
the years between wars as Manchester advances,
not knowing how they are to be enclosed.

The Vicar and the Rag and Bone Man

He looks, and beholds a pale horse
that trots past consecrated ground,
rising from his half-demolished parish.

Brick dust and splinters fly in the faces
of four angels—air and vacancy
church light irradiates into form –

who, higher than the half-completed flats,
survey interiors wet with rain,
staircases climbing to the open.

At corners the rag and bone man rides
into vacated feelings, and reoccupies them.
Legs and arms tangle on his cart.

His rags remember bones: shaped to their contours;
crumbs of skin cling to their clothes; a mirror,
broken, hatches dead faces in glass.

The angels sound their trumpets
above these revelations,
and predatory hearses circle the estate.

The Sick Room

A man reading *The Daily Herald*,
a woman and her pram, struggling with a bag,
a girl skipping and talking to her doll,
two workmen running in overalls –
my father jerked his hands up pushing them away
as they passed through the curtains and door over his bed.
I was five. My mother would not let me see how hard
the room was taking it. It wasted away,
worn to nothing by pedestrians filing through.
Colour was draining from the roses on the wall.
The ceiling thinned, letting in the sky.
Tarmac was emerging through the floor.
My father whitened, turning into his sheets.
One morning there were street noises behind the door.
The city repossessed the room, swept the curtains back.
Distances entered. Passing through there now,
the room's been worn to a pavement by the feet.

The Influence

The gull's cries are weakening
behind the gas-fire. Soot on its cramped wings,

its small black eyes in the dark –
I lose myself sympathising.

The roots of influenza tickle my throat,
its wet petals open in my nose;

my pillow's moist and torn, my face
turning to water mingled with feathers –

a passenger who rubs his eyebrow on the window,
snuggling against distances.

It's growing dark this evening
in my chest and I'm afraid –

a small pool when the tide approaches.
As sleep swallows me I try to concentrate,

to hold my shape: a slug salted
and dispersing under the rain,

a high building of mirrors and windows
mutable as weather it reflects,

the cries of flight below me.
I'm seeping into my mattress –

the fire will skirl, by morning, over emptied sheets
scalloped by my tosses and turns.

Outskirts, Inroads

The town climbs down from its valley sides
and peters, A-road wide, into petrol stations;
the road and houses shelving press her
against the wooded hill, whose population
spills into her house, whose children drop,
microscopic, from her ceiling's pores;
the wood is creeping inward down her drains.

The trees press close with August
and caterpillars, and her nipple seeps –
a cat is crying among the nests.
A tree has climbed behind her sink,
its sap branches darkly in the wall;
her armchairs harbour crevices like guilt,
gnawing and scratching nested in foam.

Too near her baby this proliferating:
slugs in the cool under cupboards
trailing albumen; hair sprouting
on carpets out of seeds from her scalp;
these rounds of killing and fertility,
of cleaning—wrigglings to life in crannies,
and the ad-man's house-worker homunculi.

Parrot

Among the dust he remembers rain-forest
where a tree falling is disastrous
for a minute—thunders for silent miles.
    Come back Peter

But life, especially insect life, goes on:
tides of ants, continual cicada,
and all the cycle of decay and growth.
    Fly away Peter

He perches on the television.
Rush hours pass in both directions
and between them buses circle around her.
    Come back Peter

Newspapers and milk accumulate,
echolalia from the streets in this silence
but nothing stays the same but her –
    Fly away Peter

—whose clock sweeps through a single season,
electrically constant, whose memories
repeat themselves in all her rooms.
　　　Come back Peter

Litter grows on nettles in her garden
which children run around unscolded,
their clothes picking up and dropping seeds.
　　　Fly away Peter

Sun invading alters her expression,
pollen is tumbling into her eyes:
look there, look there, her irises!
　　　Who's a pretty boy, now?

Verlaine in Salford

> *'One November night a few years before the turn of the century
> Paul Verlaine had lectured in a room close to the school. One can
> only wonder now what the audience made of him and he of a
> district as grim as any around the Rue Mouffetard.'*
> 　　　– Robert Roberts, *The Classic Slum*

Sleet and the sunset smoking; in my carriage,
a boy his age whose hair lifts with lice.
My window goose-pimples with water—rubbed,
it bristles with chimneys, as responsive
as skin, and vulnerable –
tormented by the drops shaken by motion.

My mother's foetuses, called Pleasure
and Chastisement, dream my double life,
mooning in a basement under alcohol:
the shamed voluptuousness of scratching; sharp nails,
on the one hand, and long soothing fingers
on the other, of the searchers for lice –

to be in Salford, not in quandary!

Its backward and forward maleness of looms
the length of the tempting night; and I
straightened and narrowed in cotton,
of Northern faith and upright standing, purged of the fires
by smoke, and snow, melting, falling on it,
the six-day sacrament and the cold showers.

Happy the Man

Alone but for Adam and Eve in yew,
Self-exiled from all parties and sects,
In my own ground I wrought the sacred cause
Higher, into the gardener's effects.

And so God's seasons, like my moods,
Were glassed in all that we had made
Until the lichens started, suddenly,
Shrivelling on the colonnade.

The glass held only me—until I was,
Not banished from the garden, but joined there:
Benches on my seat, and thoughts of others
Rippling my standing pool of air.

Glittering in the chandeliers, hazy
In the billiard room's southward view,
Manchester was looming, more substantial
Than my scagliola and ormolu.

The terrace flickered with interference,
With manmade fibres walking mongrels, ghosts
Washed up from a council estate, from air
Stirred into waves by wires and masts

—Which lifted reflections from those waves
And lined the clouds, showering traces
Not of God, across the park, but voices,
And a snow of faces melting on the leaves.

T.F. GRIFFIN

Interception

A fly buzzes around my head
In search of the centre;

My hand is moved by the energy
Of its wings to blank paper—

I am stirred by the pounding
    in my ear;
My eyes cross to a clear gaze.

The fly circles,
Its vision obscure and faultless.

I sit in motionless dialogue,
Gog the fly to Magog the brain;

I am bigger than the fly—
Its wings are thin between
    my fingers.

The fly's precocious purpose
Tests a nerve—

Soon it will land
In the centre of the desert.

The Balloon Seller

The man sold soft balloons
Of cynical thinness.
Puffing them up; letting
Them fly in all winds.

He told lies to those who
Bought them; talking
Of their cheapness, good value

And lightness.

'All men have to go to the moon,'
He sighed,
Holding the string where
The children clutched.

And he lived in down-to-earth
Town; taking home the pennies,
String and lives
Of all who thought they loved him.

Spectre

> *'Guilt is next door to innocence'* – Edwin Muir, 'Outside Eden'

You elude me again
Because you are drunk with love;
It's made me hit the stars
Until my didactic pride is torn to bits—

You call me again—
I have to go out and bite my tongue,
Cast a stone and kill a love I know is mine;
I have to shout at the sky because

You have wooed me like a partisan
When I am doubting,
Strained in guilt and willingness
Until it crumbles beyond the usual.

After this I am a man
Who has never travelled;
A guardian of my own spirit
As outwardly dead as a postbox;

You have driven me
Into the cold open blue of a question:
Who are you?
Why do you love me

When I am more outside than in?
Who cares now when the balance is tilted
And the great spectre of failure
Shapes grace into traps of meaning?

Too much knowledge drowns the sense
Into coldness:
What turns the night has taken,
What stars.

Dawn

I have caught you waking before
The full force of the day centres;

I have seen you leap high at dawn,
Testing the nerve of your spirit,

Rubbing your eyes in wonder
At the rudiment of the world.

The Pursuer

In youth, I am on a green hill;
I am the snow-cap of the black valley.
Beat, beat, speaks the brain—
I can't see you, yet I love you.

In the sun, I am vague as mountain mist;
I am speaking to the fusible air.
Beat, beat, speaks the brain—
I can't hear that you love me.

In temper, I am the cold black night;
I am the voice of the lungless life.
Beat, beat, speaks the brain—
I don't know that you love me.

In danger, I am the spineless mountain;
I am my pursuer and breaker.
Beat, beat, speaks the brain—
I know you don't love me.

In love, I am refreshed at a white lake;
I am cool soft snow-fall.
Speak, speak, says the heart—
I know you love me.

The Flower

You lend your head to a gentle beast;
A guest that grows and bends
To a doorless septum—
Bend to the light.

The world grows stars in the grass;
You are born into the very loud
And make a sceptre—
Bend to the light.

The wind seizes your scented breath
Across the sky,
Across the world—
And when you wilt

There is a way in which the sun sets
That makes the world hot to the touch.

Holiday Hotel

Alone by the sea I witness the turning of the world
Without wonderment, without moods—
Born into a clear day without myth
I am silent as before birth,
As silent as the going home.

I stay, goggle-eyed,
Anaesthetised
To the point of tears

And day by day,
Night by night,
Hotels are packed
With individuals
Who have struggled from the sea.

The Dinosaur

At night, shadowing the streets
It stood in a large mood.

Armed with hindsight it began to move
Through an ordered world.

Past the best sleeping brains,
Past electric light and moon

It lurched to find food.

Singing to the morning, to the past,
Sucking up the crumbs the night threw,
Spitting out the rusty cans
It began to grow big and heavy.

And it lurched on through ages
To become brooding; an extinction

Of mood; a pulsating pea-brain
And star.

Gathering dust for its death,
And unmovable in love for the last time

It littered doves that rose silently to power.

DOUGLAS HOUSTON

The Layman Considers the Gods of Place

What of the gods of place? Are they no more
Than rumoured reasons for how men behave?
If real, they've got a lot to answer for,
Like crying *Havoc* while Herr Hitler raved
Until the *Deutsches Volk* latched onto myth
So zealously that all good sense was sunk
In brute oblivion seeping from the pith
Of fabled boughs that crazed them power-drunk
Until their local hatred quickly seized
Upon the feared and dark minorities.
The Irish *deii loci* aren't good news;
The ethnic's heady brew when times are tough.
What native peace place can afford's abused
Till, blood-sick, gods at last cry out *Enough*.

Indigence

Rain has put an end to my work. I grub no more
In the nail-soiling earth deracinating weeds
In the large front gardens of the retired gentry,
But leap in the lane beneath the high hedges
That will soon supply me with berries and filberts,
For summer is surely ended, and though I starve
This winter, my season of labour is over.
I will go on sleeping in the flimsy outhouse
I have occupied these seven years; shooting stars
Amuse me through its open end when autumn comes
With the Perseid showers scattering sky-silver.
I celebrate my improvidence by singing
A song about chickens I learned as a boy.
The wet wood on my fire hisses like steady rain.
It chars before it burns, then quickly goes to ash.
Not much heat here, nor is my straw unduly clean,
Renewed each week from the adjacent cowshed.
I grow old, and shall not last much longer at this,
Expecting no successor in this neighbourhood.

Travelling Musician

Recalling the details fascinates me.
I see the beach where my wife and I fought,
The bedded hulks, the ocean behind us.

She went. Grief splayed like sprung steel. I wallowed
In snow, got scotch in a cheap painted glass.
My Catholic grandmother had one like that.

I dabbled a while in patent medicines.
Speciously worded, the labels' fine print
And credulous faces are crisp as stamps.

Nothing is really forgotten; I played
By cinemas, on pavements everywhere,
Four strings vibrant round the core of a song.

I played where the best whores danced—such slit skirts!
Such well propped breasts! Some money was easy,
But most of it came slowly in small coin.

Of my several wives, each beautiful,
One made good bread, another played the drums.
The note I was is fading to a pause.

The Others

I am not the man who sits alone
At a rustic table in a pub garden,
But as he turns his head to watch me pass
I admire his solitary love of air.

The man who always knows when leap years are,
Whose papers are all in immaculate order,
Is more of a stranger—aloof, I suspect,
So I call him *The Pocket Book of Boredom*.

Others constitute a powerful faction;
Their numbers are not to be taken lightly
In assessing the management of a life.
Study one or two, but keep your distance.

Their variety is overwhelming.
How they united I don't know,
But the undertaker's assistant,
Tactful as rollers under a coffin,

Delicate girls who work in flower shops,
Every Chinese person in the world,
All those who wear uniforms or nothing,
Are beyond my first person singular.

Despite occasional hostilities,
By and large they have been good to me.
Lately I agree with them on many points,
Though I hear of their internal differences.

It is my hope that these will be resolved.
I'd be foolish to take this for granted,
Each of them finally in my position,
Having seen nasty behaviour, some of it mine.

Horst Wessel on Alcatraz

My look alike passed muster in the morgue.
I left him my name. They took up the song
That impelled the metronomic goose-step
Down boulevards rippling red and black.
Disappearing quickly was expensive.
New papers and a passage fixed in Köln,
I left others to arrange the details:
The gutter nexus of crime and politics
Accepted a nominal sacrifice.
War was building while I learned American
In cinemas across the States. Newsreels

Amazed me with my name, in Denver first
In 'thirty-three, the explanations brief.
Me, the ultimate martial elegy's
Subject! What slender pretexts art requires.
I got to 'Frisco, organised some girls,
Was doing well but crossed the wrong people.
That day the splintering door was no surprise.
I'd slept with the Schmeisser all week; one burst
From under the bedclothes finished them.
I wasted time cleaning their billfolds out;
The cops were in before I'd tied my shoes.

Three paces cross this cell at its widest.
Maybe the first year is the worst: I cracked,
Fought warders, and was thrown in the hole.
After days on slops in total darkness
I couldn't tell sleep from being awake.
That song became the music of nightmares.
I begged, like guys do sooner or later;
Stark naked, I crawled when they let me out.
The warders who know I'm German taunt me
With the war—as if it was my damned fault.
Dense mist blanks out the bay again tonight.
The seagulls and foghorns sound like lost souls.
To the flat rhythm of patrolling steps
My tune is whistled on the next landing.

Devotions

Having mortified myself with a hangover,
Deliberately conceived on two days' hard drinking,
I am standing underneath the end of the pier
In the year's high ritual of my seagull worship,
Which demands such unbreakfasted, humbling rigours
And will culminate with prostration in the surf
After the solemn dispensation of breadcrusts.

A friend, long of the behaviourist persuasion,
Calls worship a proper respect got out of hand,
The mystery of the gulls beyond his dissections
To trace why what is done is done just as it is –
A closed-circuit, tape-loop mentality to me,
Only to be envied the comfort of closed doors
And confidence in the given human reasons.

He laughs at the Botanical Salvationists
Whose resurrection is the pot-plant of one's choice,
But I'd become a *nephrolepsis exalta*
Sooner than a name unsought in some register,
And their watering rites have great delicacy.
I have given him a pectoral of feathers,
And wait for him to bow, like the dove, to the gull.

I have time for Devotees of Telegraph Poles.
Sighting along their black totems at certain stars,
They believe light is soluble in midnight rain,
That high winds snatch beams from outlying farmhouses
And anglers' lamps, then mix the stuff into wet air,
Which the poles absorb to transmit the stars their light.
A simple religion, but lacking daylight truth.

I have risen now, soaked and icily refreshed,
From the white fringes of the sea where I have lain
The required fifteen minutes. Their cries above me
Worked sacred hypnosis, each mew a blade of truth.
Some of the sand from my clothes and skin will be kept
To be rubbed in my beard every Monday, run through
My fingers daily until next year's renewal.

Ward Seven
(for Bill Cooper)

Lurching out of anaesthetics
On tubular Health Service beds,
Some will now require prosthetics
Or bags that drip to keep them fed.

Counting trains and feeding pigeons,
An amputee can still react
To the world that once he lived in
Before he signed the standard pact:

More years, less pain, terms understood
For his abridgement at mid-thigh;
No clause, though knives and wills are good,
Can guarantee that no one dies.

Each beyond his own salvation,
Their democratic suffering breeds
A politics of supplication,
To each according to his needs . . .

The Return

>   *'Aujourd'hui l'espace est splendide'* – Baudelaire

The poet led me out along the quays
Where night discloses luminous desires,
Like neon leeches twitching their small fires
In cisterns of original disease.

There was no speaking in that dismal peace;
Looks asked and answered all there was to know.
The air was static as the vaulted stone
That fixed the limits where all sequence ceased.

My guide politely nodded his *adieu,*
Then, stepping into shadow, disappeared.
Escape was not as hard as I had feared;
I followed clues of light that filtered through

A dim expanse of culverts and canals.
I first saw day through grilles, then over walls;
Paved banks gave way to grass, where waterfalls
Accompanied the birds in spring chorales.

Cycle

The floor of the court of judgement splits.
The judge is jarred awake and cries
'There are specific gravities to be considered!'
The dust of the destruction drifts,
Germinates order among the primitives
Emerging from vegetable ease
On sundry planets. Men resembling men
Begin to notice their shadows,
Occur to themselves in separate forms
From which the lexicons develop,
Until the pod of structure bursts.
The floor of the court of judgement splits.

Another Time

'Another time has other lives to live' – W.H. Auden

The fantastic balloons broke free of their moorings,
Making coloured havoc in an inky sky.
Light aircraft attempted to herd them together.
In sunlight that came through beneath the building cloud
The fields we ran across were bright as summer makes them,
And scattered with bone-white tribes of mushrooms.
The eruption of smoke that filled
A quarter of the horizon
Formed into no shape of demon,
But rose to swell its own ascending turbulence.

A country where little boys were called *master*
Failed to meet the last blackmail payment.
A body politic dissolved into the world.
Some of its lighter pieces we brought here with us;
Ambition is purely local now
Interest has lost its sense of direction,
And only necessity really remains.

We made glass by melting sand.
Blotched and coarse, it admits light.
Here by the ocean I glean mussels from the rocks.

Sic Transit

The glory of the world is passing already
With white blossoms dropping from the may's laden boughs.
The heels of the man with shattered knee-caps crush them
To a moist translucency. Dead prisoners gather
On the green outside the Methodist Hall to hear
A moving address on human rights delivered
By a visiting Belgian milkman, who breaks down
When whispers inform him of a lost football match.
People who happened to be listening to radios
Maintained their politic silence while descending
To shelters now crowded and firmly closed.

Beethoven's Fifth

There will be quiet after all these deaths,
When all the toppled headstones turn to light.
The trumpet's blast takes all the angel's breath
Before he drops it laughing at the sight
Of every face distraught with hope and fear;
And suddenly the dance of heaven breaks out
With huge benevolence and peasant cheer,
All war and anger gathered in a shout
That burns itself out brightly in deep space,
While wheeling in ascent the dance expands,
All movement lit to speed by cosmic grace.
The galaxies without cannot withstand
This nebula's attraction as it grows.
All light tracks in. A single body glows.

Cemetery

The fairground's muted racket reaches here.
Shrieks of the loudest girls rise on the bass
Of rides, rock music and the ghost train's keen.

Beyond offence or reverence
The pure zero of immortality
Is silence to the massed rustle of leaves.

I saw two women laughing here today,
But now the sun is red amid the trees.
Evening's chill moral has tightened my jaw.

The Conference of Anonymity

Partially concealed within pin-stripe suits,
Special pleadings for dolphins bore us.
The dots on our brogues are more interesting
Than the relative supremacy of proximate species.

Our differences too apparent, some uniform adjusts.
Their *svelte* sameness is simple unity. No wonder
Conformity is ease. We try, reach agreement
On certain points. Don't talk of bees or killer whales.

Such creatures live with the Buddha's dullness;
No sparks between them and the world at large.
Though necessary in the last analysis,
We can learn nothing from them but peace.

After all, we can confer immanence
On tins, lend barnacled stones the power
Of knowing for our own brief purposes.
Indeed, gentlemen, we have variety at our disposal.

Driver

When vanity leaves me, I am truly alone.
I observe a nocent rendezvous of police cars,
Know each man a sort of wheel-gripping animal
Driving through the city's sodium-yellow A-roads,
My own compass set for the marshy coastal flats.
Out there I will be quite at ease, and shivering,
If this refrigerated summer has its way.
If I see Will o' the Wisp, I will write and tell you,
Otherwise consider my silence salutary.
Rubber soles dry, pedal contact excellent,
My headlights dust moth wings out past the town,
And cruising at sixty miles an hour I think of you,
Sweeter than all the chocolate on the road, more shapely
Than the slow curve of the highway out here
Where they followed the solid levels on the map .
To swing long waves of tarmac to the sea; almost there,
I believe I can smell the chosen patch of marsh.

The Rural Muse

Here there are all varieties of rain,
Some fine as mist, plenty of spattering drops,
Dense hedges that resent the hidden roads
That tortuously thread the countryside.
I am given facts of green, not ideas,
The alien silence of fields and sky
In the spaces between their background noise
Of the creatures and the leaf-rustling wind,
Or glum parables of stark containment,
Like several frogs trapped in the garden tank
Where a drowned mouse floats till all are tipped out.
No, it does not make me think, this valley,
Half way down which rain drums like hard boiling
On the thin roof of the lean-to kitchen.
Her green fist in my throat, the rural muse
Would have me believe nature is enough.

MARGOT K. JUBY

Hochzeitsmahl: 28th April 1945

Married in black is bad,
but apt;
his favourite silk.

Berlin is burning.

And we are in a tight net
closing.
I am very happy.

I came here of my own free will
to be with him –
to die, not to be married.

In front of everyone he kissed me
full on the mouth:
it made me very happy.

This is the end of everything.

Where are the little bridesmaids?
Sleeping:
fast asleep, they missed the wedding.

Tomorrow we must kill the dog:
he knows this
and it makes him sad.

See that the paraffin is ready:
prepare the bridal bed.

Although this night may be the last
he always loved me:
he has made me happy.

I am Frau Hitler now
and proud –
tell my mother I was married.

Hand me the poison.
Hand me the pistol.
Leave us alone together, please.

And if you see my mother –
tell her this –
when last you saw me, I was very happy.

Dominoes at 'The Polar Bear'

A good game, this, for Sunday nights
when some of us have to get up in the morning.

Between two, it is intimate:
a courtship ritual with bones and coins.

Three is a crowd and more is interesting:
the drink slides down, the coins change hands.

The bones rattle.
It is a Sunday like other Sundays.

The weekend has bled away as weekends do –
blood from a severed jugular.

There is nothing unusual.
A tension in the air, perhaps.

A blurring of outlines –
nothing to worry about, nothing at all.

But who holds which domino?
This is the question, one of many questions.

Nothing is clear:
you cannot blame the beer, not altogether.

The eyes, so many eyes, everyone's eyes –
shuttered windows, one-way mirrors.

What have they got to hide?
We are all friends here, are we not?

There are no knives under the table.
The ritual proceeds with coin and bone.

'But whose side are you on?'
Mine, friend. Not yours: not his: not hers.

A ceremony of love or blood.
Sharper than Aztec knives our weapons.

Who has control of the game?
Does anyone know what game we are playing?

And what exactly are we playing for –
are the stakes too high?

There is more to lose than coins on a table.
Forget the rules, friend: play to win.

Love Lore

A drop of menstrual blood in his drink
is the female trick:
much harder for men –
they have to soak nail-parings,
cut their thumbs,
and neither way seems quite as good.

The Romans knew it all, of course,
feasting on shellfish, octopus, mullet,
electric ray:
if all that failed
plying their loves with spices: pepper, myrrh.

Lucretius killed himself, they say,
frenzied by some elixir:
magicians of Thessaly peddled drugs

potent enough to drive men crazy.

Cantharides, the famous Spanish fly,
should be used in moderation;
not many years ago, two women died
retching convulsively –
victims of some man's urgent lust.

Use it only in desperation:
at worst it causes vomiting,
sears the internal organs,
can be fatal –
but use it, use it if you must.

The phallic mandragora,
Circe's plant,
works wonders, by repute;
if you can bear the maddening scream
that tears your brain as you uproot it.

Cowards can wear magnetic amber
or ivy at the breast:
vicious ladies can knot the aiglet,
render him limp as the string they tie,
unfit for any other woman's bed.

Or you could try the obvious –
powdered rhinoceros-horn,
stags' genitals
and everything symbolic.
Still, there is only one infallible . . .

First, catch your unicorn.

Haiku

Your gloves are scarlet,
woman's gloves in soft leather –
did your wife choose them?

Bluebeard

Bluebeard turns the key and remembers:
turns the key
to lock the dead ones in.

And there they lie
dismembered,
fresh or withered, stiffened and helpless:
Bluebeard shakes with fear.

They had to die,
he says,
I had to kill them –
but not for curiosity.

Curiosity kills no cats,
nor women neither.
Legend lies.

Bluebeard remembers – long ago –
the first of many who lay beneath him,
virgin, waxen,
with trembling smile.

After his passion
eyes like a doe's
gaze up disappointed:
'Is that all? Is that all?'

So many times he forgets the faces.
They rot behind locked door
and dripping walls.

Bluebeard yearns for a real woman –
princess, peasant,
even a whore;
a woman to moan and cry beneath him,
a woman to make him a man.

Bluebeard never doubts his manhood:
safe from the tattling tongues
his knife has stilled
he turns the key.

But through his frigid castle
echoes the taunting cry:
'Is that all? Is that all?'

The Grey Man

He is a web of milky semen
spread on the air to strangle the unwary:
I hang there, only half reluctantly.

His hands are twin white spiders in my mind.
My breasts are withered by their touch –
no other hand will rest there for a while.

He is the third at every lovers' meeting,
the absence that turns tenderness to dust:
I've seen his breath make candles flicker.

He is the valley of the shadow –
I creep along in his grey atmosphere
numbed by the cold and taking on his colour.

He is the fog, pervading and polluting:
bone of a dead thing, bleached by rain:
the face that ages in my mirror.

I'd cut my wrists, but he would drink the blood.

Lebensraum

I could be happy here, I think,
if only things would let me be.

This was the servants' quarters once,
a house in miniature, all the angles wrong.

The furniture's mine, I'm self-contained
and the rent is suspiciously low.

Here I can play at keeping house,
disturbed by a sense of actually belonging.

This is my lebensraum, my Poland;
I'm almost inclined to think of it as home.

Slugs trace their ciphers in the hall
and outside swims the lush aquatic garden.

I could sit with you in a haze of June
drunk on the ghost of elderberry wine.

The berries not yet picked, nor ever will be,
but you wouldn't mind.

There would be whisky in the cupboard,
beer in the fridge, upstairs a double bed.

I could keep a cat, a mangy grey,
lean and mean as the men I've loved.

I know I could be happy here
if things would let me be.

Offering

A triple candle-flame is bright enough
to love by:
mirrors magnify the light.

The triple moon attains her potent full:
throned in Cancer
she rules supreme.

The lunar pull is strong tonight.

Women miscarry;
rivers overflow;
the fluids of the brain flood through the cortex;
there will be murders done in this dead light.

October, too, the month of harvest:
a sickle wet with blood,
a sacrifice;
the hungry moon demands her victim.

I light three candles.
You are grey as bone.

My face stares blankly from the mirror,
a bloodless mask,
the eyeslits black with kohl.

We have the same desires,
the moon and I.

Glint of an earring,
glint of a tooth:
silver and ivory, metal and bone.

The moon is gazing avidly at you
and you are caught between her eye and mine
and I am ready now –
are you?

'Mirror, Mirror . . .'

My mirror has its ebbs and flows;
goes by the moon
like my blood, like the sea.

Over your shoulder you can glimpse
a mask of the devil (so preachers say)
mocking female vanity.

Or at Hallowe'en gaze eagerly and see
a husband, a lover –
a pallid coffin.

An overhead light will show your future:
daylight is kinder.
Mirrors are liars.

Tonight my reflection's in masculine mood.
I search in vain for the woman I am:
there is the man I was, or will be.

At other times the skull beneath the skin:
tonight, the shadow behind the substance:
dream, not reality.

The man within me mimes each female move:
my breasts, my flowing blood
a hollow joke.

Like a chrysalis
he broke me open:
from the safe side of glass he stares at me.

Tomorrow my woman's face, or the coffin:
tonight I'll dream a mirror-world,
the secret underside of waking.

And a shadow will always follow me.

SEAN O'BRIEN

Late

In the rented rooms above the bay
The simmer of epistles was like sleep.
Old men grow bored with young men's books,
But still they followed and were sold
At the stall that an uncle had kept.
His landlady found roses in the hall
Without a note, and for the afternoon
There was the itch of Sundays at the Spa:
Band-music, marble, heat and wickedness.
He did not have to work, she thought.
Eat greens for the conduct; wear sensible shoes;
Keep up with the journal; walk out to the light
At the pier's end, a mile in the ocean.
Look back for the window seen only from here.
It is only a place you can see.
It survives you. It makes you a ghost,
Where she lived, where we both lived once.
I am embarrassed to have stayed
So long and on so little and for this.

The Disappointment
(for Stuart Ross and John Pettenuzzo)

The sky becomes mother-of-pearl,
A lady's box of trinketry.
Inside it the air can remember
Lavender at two removes,
Like someone's love once dreamed about
But not possessed, and longed for now.

In one of these burgherly houses,
Room on room on corridor,
It is someone's finale, unpacking herself
From lint and pins and looking-glasses.
Not even the letters are cryptic here,
But bland with young 'accomplishment',

Valuable only in histories of boredom:
Chat of some dud couple caught
In frames where time stands in for love,
With their backs to a sea to whose ironclad rightness,
Decked with pennants, fleet on fleet,
They bore unthinking witness. They were cold.

All afternoon I trudge around
Inventing tasks. I look and sniff
And find Victoria and Albert
Brilliant white and everpresent.
High on windy plinths The Great outstare
The disappointment of their will

As dusk elaborates the park.
A duck-guffaw, a lacy hem of frost,
A salesman reading *Penthouse* in his car,
Pianoforte being taught and loathed –
Its sweet unwarranted effects,
Not brave enough for sorrow but still there.

The Brochure

Built for bracing airs above the sea,
It shadows half the beach
And mines the sandstone cliffs with larders
Red brick, grey brick, yellow corners, square
And grosser than the national product.
Admire the glass-eyed Nemo-domes
And sawn-off fire-escapes
On the locked heights.
Behind the screams of hooded gulls
The screams of doomed remittance-men:
Behind them both, the rubber tread
Of floor-detectives, rigorously picked
From jails and noncommissioned ranks.
Their doctors' bags are pursed
For pliers, greaseproof packets,
The complete range of fillings,

Toenails, St Christopher medallions,
Postal orders, things in lockets,
Promises extracted on notepaper
Headed *The Grand*, plus the various
Snifters of morphine, the various
Samples of semen and blood.
Minute attention is their mark,
While lower down in sweating kitchens
Waiters redirect the pipes
To the bottling plant. At the cocktail hour
Fine goblets of urine appear
On silver trays on tables at the doors
Of virgin brides: beneath each glass,
Lubricious propositions, costed.
Following dinner, the dancing with swords
And the drawing of lots for the novelty gangplank,
The raffle of the pickled parts, the old songs.
Be assured that none is excluded.
In case there is an enemy
The highly trained homunculi
Who staff our deep torpedo rooms
Will fire you from sewer-pipes
Across the moonlit bay.

Walking
(for Deborah)

I am in love with detail. Chestnut trees
Are fire-damaged candelabra.
Waterbirds are porcelain.
The planthouse is the room within the room
And all this is England,
Just left here, and what's to be done?

It does not remember the dances,
Silk stockings and murders and money.
We were not invited. We came late
To trespass on ourselves among the furniture,
Admiring the upholstery of Hell,
Where the talk is the best and you know it.

Adulterous cortège of cars around the park,
Where the couples are solving themselves with despair.
They will die of each other.
They have names, they were born –
If they're held to the light they have souls,
Like little ingots knocking at the heart.

O Vaughan and Geoffrey, Annabel and Jane,
Your time is up, you've gone professional:
You are condemned to live this script
Until the gestures make you retch,
And then forever, knowing it –
The passive yes, the nominated self,

The grammar till it vanishes,
Among these great facilities,
Where she and I are walking, I believe.
We're holding hands. I say, and then repeat,
There is no nightmare big enough to hurt,
Since it fits with the tick of the gold at my heart.

The Lamp

Slowly, these evenings, it warms to its business,
Adding its ivory miniature wattage
To headaches unbidden or begged for;
To love doing overtime, vicious or civil.
A simple but brilliant composure
Of levers and springs, with a bulb and a flex,
It should be an eye but is not, and should know
But does not, and should feel but cannot.
It squats at my shoulder and silently stares,
Giving nothing away of the dreams it can't have.
These dreams concern high cold
And long views from a clinic to Europe
Set out beneath its haze of sun
And politics. No loneliness, no cry,
Can climb to the terrace where money is dying,
In rarefied purple, with desperate good humour.

The lamp is in place by the notes on the desk
In the room that is kept at the dry heat of health
And has four walls of medical journals.
Nobody lives here and no-one is missing.
Strange if when some modernist made this
He failed to see its perfect sex. Plug in, turn on
And leave alone: blank ecstasy
Unbounded by the mortal physics.
An anglepoise lamp done in white.
If you were to ask me that now I should act
In reasonable faith to find a name
For what it does, then I would have to say,
You asking me, you being you, and reason being
What it is, and the lamp being here,
A prosthetic of dark in the room,
It sheds light, I suppose. *It depends what you mean.*

Clio
(for Dave Lewis)

Arcane and absolutist aunt
Refusing access over tea,
You are my private hierophant
And you embroider me.

You say you know me inside out,
This man I haven't met,
And you could tell me all about
What hasn't happened yet.

But nothing happens here at all
As far as I can see.
The lack of pictures on the wall
Is how it's meant to be.

You have the leisure to be bored
And so you still trot out
The view that you must be adored,
Which I take leave to doubt:

Your ironies are second rate,
Imagination nil – ·
So how do you concoct my fate,
And what about this will?

You smile that smile and preen yourself
And ply me with a bun:
You were the first one on the shelf
And all you've ever done

Is recognize my vanity
And tease it till it screams,
Whilst feeling up my sanity,
The small coin of my dreams.

Gentility's as impolite
And secretive as cancer –
Both kick several shades of shite
From any life-enhancer.

Then I hear, 'Let's try again
And then you can go home.
It takes a little English pain
To build a metronome.'

So I'm reciting day and night
The masters and their grief.
I'll know when I have got it right
If boredom kills belief.

Remote and circular, your place
Evaluates my senses,
Palgrave's Golden Interface,
Dismantler of tenses,

Scholar-Critic's time machine,
Will Travel Anywhere,
Though somehow I have never been
Around when I was there.

So will you? Won't you? Should I care?
Has it ended or begun?
I do not know if I can bear
Interminable fun.

But I don't think I'll ever die.
I don't suppose you'll let me.
Every time I say goodbye
You threaten to forget me.

For Lowell George

What fills the heart is felt to make amends,
Until the flooded heart can no more choose
Release than never sing its staggered blues.
I wish you had not found such special friends.
At thirty-four, at three a.m., in bed,
Of overweight helped on by dope and booze,
Before your talent bored you you were dead.

Victorians

White heads, white hats, in garden chairs,
Enthusiasts of time,
Adulterous and hopeful men, who met
Their fallen girls at stations out of town:

This day of summer's yours in perpetuity.
I cannot love your manners or your work,
But accidental bravery persists,
In homiletic lilac and your vanity in stone.

We were the epic exegetes
And called religiose.
We are what's left when time retreats,
The syphilitic rose:

How honesty becomes opaque,
The season drawing on:
We looked into the little lake
And wanted to be gone.

Let this be noon, before the letter comes,
The daughter coughs, the verses are exposed,
Before the century goes black,
And you go blind, and all the doors are closed.

Jazz

It is to you, my dear, I owe
This love of the soloing saxophone.
You are going away, for a while.
I have borne that before.
I am only afraid
Of the highly-strung bass
Like a clock in the groin.

Le Départ

You've been leaving for years and now no-one's surprised
When you knock to come in from the weather.
The crew is past embarrassment:
They can live with their nautical names, and with yours.
So sit, take down your glass and talk
Of all that is not you, that keeps you here
Among the sentimental stevedores
In the drinking clubs in the dank afternoons
Of your twenty-ninth year. There may be news.

Indeed. Somebody drowned last night, walked sideways
Off a Polish fishmeal hulk. A rabid Paraguayan bear
Was seen among the kindly hookers eating fruit.
A hand-carved coelacanth was found

When the cells were dug out to lay drains . . .

How can you not be struck by these arrivals?
The perfect boat is sailing Tuesday week.
It's heading southwards, way beyond the ice –
Starsailing seems quite plausible by night.
Until then there is querulous Ninepin
(The loss of his ticket for thieving)
And Madeleine's never-secret grief
(Be kind, and ask politely what)
And someone selling crocodiles
And hash from the sump of a jungle . . .
Now even the Juvaro have secret accounts –
Sell them your Service Forty-Five
And get a tape-recorder back . . .
The Amazon's an answering service:
No-one's ever really lost. A month ago
Rocheteau, stuck for credit, offered up
The pelvic bones of Mungo Park
In exchange for a fifth of *Jim Beam* . . .
We always thought that Scot was lying about Africa.

It is easily night: soft boom of lighter-boats
Beyond the fogwall, swung on inauthentic tides
That left you here, that left you here
As the lovesongs go over the warehouse
Among patrolling cats and a lost A.R.P.
With his bucket of sand and his halberd.

You are doped on the stairs on the way to the moon
With Yvonne, who has aged but not quite,
Who knows the words to every song
And places one flattering palm on your spine
Till you move, who keeps a special bottle
For you (but half gone, half gone) by the bed,
A black fire of sugar that says all there is
About travelling. You're halfway there.

And all shall sing until the awful morning
Reminds them of themselves,
Then sleep in early restaurants,

Boastful of such daft endurance,
And then inspect the shipping lists
Until the time is right.

'You talk in your sleep,' says Yvonne.
'So I woke you. All this travelling –
You leave the girls for what?
Are we not always, always travelling?
Let's drink to that, and one before you go.'

Station Song

I should have seen you all the time, you ghosts,
But I was taken up elsewhere
With getting on, which got me here.
I'm back for good. You are
So patient, like the best of hosts.

Am I your guest?
The girl, is she one too?
You say there's nothing I must do,
That I am not accountable to you.
You wish me nothing but the best.

I try to see if I'll get lost.
I walk the streets. But then a sign
Propped up on bricks explains what's mine:
One door along this line
Of doors that open on to dust.

The Snowfield

It is so simple, being lonely.
It's there in the silence you make
To deny it, the silence you make
To accuse the unwary, the frankly alone.

In the silence you bring to a park
When you go there to walk in the snow
And you find in the planthouse,
Next to the orchids in winter slow-motion
And the sleeping unreadable mosses,
Sick men, mad, half-born, who are sitting
As long as the afternoon takes.
Left there by helpers hours ago,
As if preparing for a test,
Each holds a book he cannot open.

Some days you put together
Sentences to say for them
As you leave to go back to the street.
With work they might be epigrams
Of love and modest government.
And this thought frees you. You pick up the paper.
You eat. Or you go to the library and talk.

But some days there is nothing
You cannot know. You still leave,
But it seems to take hours, labouring
Back to the street through the snowdrifts
And not worth the effort.
It seems that this is all there is.
It happens like snow in a park, seen clearly
After days of admiration, and looking
As if it had always been there, like a field
Full of silence, that is not beginning or ending.
It is so simple. You just hadn't looked.
And then you did, and couldn't look away.

The Park by the Railway

Where should we meet but in this shabby park
Where the railings are missing and the branches black?
Industrial pastoral, our circuit
Of grass under ash, long-standing water
And unimportant sunsets flaring up

Above the half-dismantled fair. Our place
Of in-betweens, abandoned viaducts
And modern flowers, dock and willowherb,
Lost mongrels, birdsong scratching at the soot
Of the last century. Where should we be
But here, my industrial girl? Where else
But this city beyond conservation?
I win you a ring at the rifle range
For the twentieth time, but you've chosen
A yellow, implausible fish in a bag
That you hold to one side when I kiss you.
Sitting in the waiting-room in darkness
Beside the empty cast-iron fireplace,
In the last of the heat the brick gives off,
Not quite convinced there will be no more trains,
At the end of a summer that never began
Till we lost it, we cannot believe
We are going. We speak, and we've gone.
You strike a match to show the china map
Of where the railways ran before us. Lost
Coal and politics, invisible decades
Of rain, domestic love and failing mills
That ended in a war and then a war
Are fading into what we are: two young
Polite incapables, our tickets bought
Well in advance, who will not starve, or die
Of anything but choice. Who could not choose
To live this funeral, lost August left
To no one by the dead, the ghosts of us.

The Name

Vlad the Impaler, the torturer's horse,
And the mercantile towers of Asia
Stacked with skulls like death's exchequer.
Something must be done with Sunday:
Florid libraries deputize for God.
When the light has run back through the page
I can hear the wind gathering leaves,

But one name in the cursory millions
Has lodged like a seed in my throat.
Katya, whom Anonymous has praised
Forgettably for being young and his
In summer thirteen twenty-six.
This is only a way of repeating her name,
A charm, that can't believe in time.
The wine my conscience drinks tonight
Can run as sweet and harsh as hers
Across my tongue. These apples cannot weigh
So firm and cool upon my hands.

TONY PETCH

Cider-making in Herefordshire

In a bad year cider is made of stones.
Blood in the apples means more deaths,
Hinges are squeakier, mother has washday ribs
And the ploughman gets drunk on peelings.
The jiggery-pokery of rigor mortis
Is stumped by felling and blunt pruning,
But there's no time to be upset.
When you have to get on with it
Hard work is nursed through thick and thin
Despite the ones the next storm takes with it.
As the poor take another bite their crisp mouths shrink
But the alcohol runs on through the century
To thirsty days of a sweeter kind.
Once all the bungling is cobbled together
And a boot is put in the mouth of the earth
A well-heeled beverage is on the way,
Its fruit in harness, the body between the shanks.
Shafts of sunlight creak under each cart of ripeness
While the drunk wheel trundles on in a rough cider rut
To where the waggoner dumps his squeaky load
And leaves a short-cut silence behind him.
He hasn't much to say to the women
Who fill the oxwain by the basketful.
Balancing on flimsiness, the leaves gossip
As whispers are smuggled in through the branches,
But there's not a lot of elbow-room in the crown
Where the Hagloe Crab is held in high esteem.
By the time the pickers have finished their hands have vanished.
Then the trees are hit with polting lugs
And the mason smooths down the grinder
So colour is tightened and the kernel is hit.
What is batted back with a wooden spatula
Lodges at the edge in these engines of pungency.
The machines look pretty. At the festival of pressing
A noisy horse makes the cogs go
Jerking the teeth on the axle so the orchard is crushed
Till it gets boring in leather and chains

And each nut, pip, and bolt gets a mention.
Even the moon is squeezed with a belt
So its last bit of light plops in the liquid.
Midnight excites it: its brightness escapes and shines on.
In a brewer's landscape the rind of the district,
Plus core, stalks and all, change the flavour.
Every grower is known by his fruit:
Pauson, Royal Wilding, Golden Pippin, Dymmock Red.
The Stire puts a bloom on the cheeks
While the Redstreak draws from a deep strong land.
Getting the casks right is important,
The rougher workings rarely filled to the bung,
And there are several rackings before blood is added.
When a shoulder is stuck in the vat the meat dissolves
Just as the odd dead rat makes the drink taste better,
And agitated fluid ferments earlier
With a rosy prospect caught in the booze.
Two hogsheads is a good day's labour
For ciderists drunk on the proceeds.
When the church bells are asunder at harvest
And worship is no longer marketable
Another skinful of history's dizzy with bubbles,
The excess plonked in the font.
Though good times last longer from bottles, it's not all like this.
In a bad year cider is made out of stones.

From the Papers

Townsfolk described by the flowers that they grew,
Species ranked neatly in order of class.
Scores on the cricketfield, bat hitting ball,
Mention of laughter, and words of applause.
Doorbells in High Streets rung late in the night,
Rumours of Hoskyns and Mary and Fred.
Colours of bunting to celebrate peace,
And prices of cattle, new milk and hay.
Stories of people run over by carts,
Sickness and innocence, census returns.
Sideshows in detail, fun on the swings,

Boys with their fingers in cogs of machines,
Lockjaw in hospital. Poor little things,
Birthdays on weekdays that end with the world.
Tramps put in prison for stealing a hen,
Court scenes and errors and too much to drink.
The lies and pronouncements, judgement and doubt,
Violent rousings, and inquests, and pain.
Long lists of graziers, paupers and lords
Buried along with their lovers and smells.
Old sounds and attitudes under the ground,
These lives completed and everything done.
But gaps in the silence are said to remain.

In the Desert

A column of water
The colour of nothing
Joins the tap
To the sand.

Tight as glass
And longer than my thirst,
My hand goes through it
And it goes through my hand.

Using my fingers
I shape it into the horse
I was riding
And let it stand.

Keeping Time

They row past on the pond behind the band,
Their oars slow wings that fan the tune,
Edwardians keeping timeless time.

Elsewhere, the needles set in air
To pace the splintering in the fire,
Knit by coal-light. And again there's no-one there.

Leaving for Home

A huddle of mountains is jostling for position on the postcard
And Di carves her signature into the parapet instead of
                              writing, 'Wish you were here'.
She's sturdy and blonde and has done her fair share of
                    kissing the bums she thinks about when it rains.
Monday morning's soap reminds her of the daredevil who
                              knocked on her windowpane
And was later found clutching the sills on floor nine of the Hilton.
Squeezed through his stomach the holiday chips would
                              look pretty nasty
Down where the traffic jam is making its way to tea and
                    Janet's red dress is caught in the rush hour.
When only the plumbing is left of this hotel and some
           futurist has put it on video for housewives in Europe
The edges of the city will be coming adrift from their moorings
And the jets won't go any further.
Where a few moths are still practising their fluttering prior to
           bashing their brains out on the moon at midnight
A map of wrecked galleons and shifting sands unfolds its
                    wings in search of more stable destinations.
With two pronouns and forty-two syllables to go
Kevin will run out of paper and the letter home will never get
                              there.
Fooling around in the bedroom, hate rolls up everything.
As fun seeps through the crevices at last and moistens the
                              rollicking people,
Pencilled eyebrows vanish over the crest of the roller-coaster
And a professor of biology relaxes anonymously in alcohol
                              and foreign languages.
It's like that, fake husbands lining the streets and leaning
                    languidly in tall entrances,
Their wives hopeful of being kissed even in the steamiest
                              of kitchens.

For yawning in forests will soon be a thing of the past
As will be nodding at the pensioners in their rickety skeletons.
They are also on vacation from the world and have long
            forgotten the days that were bonelike with algebra.
In enlarging on any of the generations it is wise to lower a few
                                    of the profiles,
For the drunk who jettisons himself from the balcony like
        a messiah or an astronaut is less likely to defy gravity.
Behaviour is very often lionesque, but that doesn't mean
                        Kevin will miss the bullet,
Only that Di or Janet is more likely to get in the way of the
                                    next one
Just as being rich is more fattening if you've still got your teeth in.
Hilly dinners are supposedly the envy of any Marxist
Or envoi of frazzled lovers able to boast well about their
                        marbles as they reach for the wine.
Whenever you cut one of these sparkling evenings open
                    and sunlight flops out of its shell
The guests find themselves sliding about dreamily on pearls
                                    of stupidity
Clouds under siege from thunder squeeze an aroma of
                    apricot out of the stratosphere
And petals, food, oil and semen drop through chinks in
        the stadium where Kevin and Di are marvelling at the
                                    death of a bull.
Throughout the storm, Janet the dancer is pouting her lyrics
                                in the nightclub
As potty anagrams and a blue leotard are committed to memory.
Meanwhile the native population are salvaging their
                        children with savagery.
As shoplifters they are often a little subservient,
While as looters they are always silly for ages afterwards.
Nipples caught in the act of procreation and lips just as they
                                    are opening
Mean that the guilty immediately hanker after some sort
                        of retrospective salvation.
It's only that we're one world war nearer the next one
And that the gunnery of the nervous group of mercenaries
                            up front is still imperfect.
They are still chasing the pock-marked escapologist long after
        he completed his train journey back to university.

A bottle of pressed grapes is left poking out of his luggage,
But the cornfield that was meant for the professorial
                              packing-case never got harvested.
His two-pronged fantasies are all very well,
But changing sex on your way back from the poop-deck
                              when you are still suffering jetlag
Is of no consequence to the likes of Kevin and Janet who
      are struggling to get their cosmetics from the quayside
                                          to the quadrangle.
Sometimes the place where the boat docks has a lighthouse
                .   and there used to be a pier there.
Being gentle always ought to be done sideways,
From the top or underneath the swirls are fortuitous
Even for those who return brown as a berry to peer back
                        overseas through holes in the autumn.
Few stings are soothed with lotions on the world's best airlines,
But there will always be enough flesh left over for fooling
                        around in gold lanes on early closing.
Although being noble and behaving like a whizz-kid by
                  having one foot hard down on the accelerator
Is one of the best ways to miss the main point of the argument,
Only by looking forward in the pub at Sunday lunchtime to
            fast cars and reminiscing about her teetering frolics
Will Di get well soon enough to be off again with Janet
                        and Kevin, this time on horseback.

Mushrooming

Mushrooming by moonlight,
The burglar of quiet fungi
Creeps on crêpe grass
With a straw bag.

Before he picks them
He touches them
To see how they feel.

Before he picks them
He makes sure
The moon is the only one watching,

That only the moon
Is permitting him
To have so many mistresses
In one night.

The Owl

The owl hollows his hoot out of old oak,
And when he puts on the boot of his flight
I feel so comfortable on his back.

His search for mice
Is as if they were stars in his cat's-eyes.

Though his feathers ache,
He keeps his wings and feet fit with gymnastic equipment.

When the doorbell goes
It is either the milkman, the paperboy or the postman.
It will not be the owl.

The Advancement of Knowledge

My grandfather kept stars.
Sussex stars. The last of the breed.
They were good layers,
Ghost stars giving birth
To ghosts.

When he was hungry
He would wring their necks
Somewhere in the nettles.

In the village school
Where I learned to count ghosts
And nettle stings on my fingers
Is a picture of a chicken –
And a star.

Nocturne
(for Peter Didsbury)

From pollen in the lunar orchard
Ripeness falls like silver onto lawns.
A bitten shiny fruit with crescent bruises
Keeps its fist of flavour in its skin.
How cool it is and high up when I pick them
In apple hatcheries where pips are born,
Pippin moons from which the whole crop spins.

GENNY RAHTZ

Hull

You may watch
How the River Hull
Slides her barges leeward
To the Humber
And shows these empty pods
A wedge of shadow
Sunk beneath their bows.

And the paddle steamer
With the red and black funnel
Still rides her half-circle
Round sandbanks to New Holland
To return, for a follower
Of her passage,
Abstracts of all her movements.

These routine passages of the eye
Belong to waterways
Whose tides leave their bloom
To silt the docks
And whose remnants of full use
Are warehoused
In semi-shrouded lots
On museum streets.

As yet there are no picture-postcards
Of these sights,
No more arranged to be visited
Than the old men
Who may be photographed
When they lie asleep,
Or the groups of boys
Seen fishing from the path
Of warehouse yards.

So attend this subdued city
Providing for its livelihood

Not its looks,
And keep what you find secret
From all obliterating praise.

Thunderstorm

Two warm eggs,
We are all smooth anonymous limbs.
My small son enfolds a part of me,
Foetal yet separate.

We lie awake
Waiting for the split of light,
The immersion of sound
That cracks open our breathing.

Beach

Recognition of debris
And the smell of dry popping seaweeds . . .
We leave them lying in ant-sand
And crouch over pebbles
To subtract the odd piece
Of wet colour.

This beach can sand us down
To a clean grain.
We want its great age and offerings
And impersonal pounding
To lap our brains
In this brief landscape.

But nerve impulses
Vary their pace
And destination,
Acting as unique latch-keys
To release those cerebral events

That we call naming . . .

We stake out these flood-plains
To expunge ourselves,
Pat smooth domes
And funnel tricklings of sand
That slump in shallow gradients
Or blow as sand dust.

Movement in the Street

I have learnt to map movement
In the street,
And walk or drive
Within these expectations.
But sometimes,
Inviolate in my tin box,
I trespass on the idea
Of exterminating
A whole nuclear family –
Cardboard cut-outs
In a pop-up book.

Nature films on television
Show that gazelles who lag behind
On the edge of the herd
Can be run down, dragged away
And eaten.

House Maintenance

I have taken a small hammer and chisel
To this putty triangle,
One side wood, one glass
And one paint.

For I am obliged by the spring

To offer my kitchen new life
And replace this winter war-glass
With clear glass:

This afternoon, a concave matchstick figure
Digs the garden. Boot on spade
Can hoist March-softened earth
From last year's spinach roots.

Here I command further triangles,
Those confined by myself using the spade
And the up-ended sections
Of wedged clay.

I will then take exact measurements
For glass, with a steel tape,
And make good
My previous labour.

Rat Catcher

I am my own rat catcher.
I let the beast go.
He is too living and large
To trap, to break his back.
I divide my own history
To accommodate this
Bleak presence
And reminder of the half-light.

I allocate whole days
For servicing this hidden life,
Feeding this enquiring rat-spirit.
I let him eat my food,
Curious at what infections
I might incur.
He is my excuse.
I tidy and clean for him.
He is the reason for my delay

In choosing
What feline company I keep.

I am waiting
For the rat to be caught
By someone else, in their traps.
They will pull its fur
From the inside of my head
And unclamp its teeth
From my will.

The Jug

Give this notice
To one flowered jug,
The cottage-bedroom variety
Rimmed with pink lustre.

They are recognized, jugs,
By the different fits
That fashion or stability
Slapped to their purpose.

Their differences allow
Concavities to match
Jug beside jug,
Find fit at weak points

For lips, parts for holding
And the tensed bowl of their stomachs.
Their eye of liquid lies
Tight as dolls' eyes

Till speech betrays
The same jugged loss
At every tilt
From equilibrium.

The Last Photograph

We become frightened
Of knowing how fast
The word 'together' holds.
Is this the last photograph
We'll ever take?
This moment feels
As if it should be memory, stamped
With a 'last look'
At your mother's rooms,
At her cupboards storing china
For her sons' brides,
For her children
When they are grown up.

Ashtray

In the café
At the Hull Ferry
There is an off-white
Hollowed disc
Of coarse pottery
Which contains
The last pressings
Of two cigarettes
And one used match.

This has its burnt point
Rubbed smooth
As if in remembrance
Of half-felt thoughts
Doodled
Like the ash
Into scratched drifts.

On these traces
Alien to their more

Vegetable nature
Is a metal parcel
Squeezed
From small pieces
Of tinfoil.

And this pronounced
As residue,
This abstract of activities
Earlier compiled,
And, like those
Beyond this window,
Since curtailed.

Poplars and Limes

There are enough smiles
Between other people
To break the days,
And summer closeness
Holds me to an absence
By my side again,
To every sun-awakened building,
Private in the streets
Where I walk.

This city shelters
For such short seasonal periods,
Poplar and lime decorated
For its reputation
As a green city,
In summer.

Poplars

Poplars slipped from their roots,
Wreaths of new issue

Sprung in delicate assault
On their winter mesh

Caught like a green soot
Sparked from hedges,
Glued with wet marrow
Fugitive from the earth.

Thus do we find relief
From wintering.
The cautious nostril, folded eye
And inattentive skin

Stretch as these shadows
Sharpen their first focus
Set by this year's splintering
Against the spring.

Id Mud

Id mud from the Humber
Skews the tide-weed,
Slumps on dock walls
And shores up those dry land
Marks of a city language.

Each part of the city
Portrays itself
By accumulation
Of double yellow lines,
Blue triangles, red circles,
Street-lamps of different arcs
And the shorthand of skyline.

Trees have the purpose here
Of city trees.
In back gardens they demarcate
Eccentric geometries
Of lapped inflexible tiles

That shoulder the self-same elements
As the leaves.

This sense of city overpowers me.
Its physicality
Persuades my movements
And would influence
The character of eyelets used
To lace this patterned cloth.

FRANK REDPATH

To the Village

Everyone, I suspect, learns his own way
To find the place: though most
Leave the main road by the transport café
Then head towards the coast,
The signposts in the by-ways are erratic,
Their placings local, idiosyncratic.

Some quite important turnings are not named;
Some that look promising
End up in paddocks or deserted farms
Or lead you in a ring
Fingered by names that don't turn into places
Through narrowing hedge-vistas with no houses.

You have to learn a litany of signs
To get you there in one –
The broken barrow and the stack of churns,
The disused harrow on
The roadside where you meet the unmarked fork.
Unplanned, impermanent. Odd that they work.

From Our Cycling Correspondent

Biking to work was a good idea. Improbable insects
Of giant yellow steel have been at work
For weeks among the slums.

They have cleared whole squares of houses, shops,
Small factories where lives were made, and furtive
Embraces. Light has been let in.

Don't jump to conclusions. List
What you can see. Here
Was some kind of an enclosure.

Two walls still stand, an arch,
In damp cold air. They say
You are here, it is now,

But not still; time is passing.
Smoke rises from ceiling joists, wigwammed
Over low piles of fallen bricks.

They burn. Flames excite themselves, the air
Shivers around them, they hurry
To tell themselves the news. We shall burn forever.

Down long broad avenues crowds run
To greet the new Shah. Explosions and laughter.
They are picnicking on the barricades.

There

To get there you have to abandon the car,
Jump over ditches, mount by sheep track
To the scree slope on the blind side of a farm or village

Where, in the silent heat, if patient
You may observe the unremarkable
Events that litter loading bays and backyards.

Such as a tin bath full of water
Afloat on cobbles, a garden fork on sentry
Stuck in the earth half-way along a row

And an open doorway. Somebody, you suppose
Went in before you came there; somebody, it's certain,
Will come out, whether you stay or go.

Or you may find yourself there, surprised,
When asking directions, for caretakers equip
Their caves with tea-cups, vacuum-flasks, calendars, and

Cleaners pin postcards from friends at the seaside
To broom-cupboard walls, and among the ledgers
Accounts clerks cherish succulents and cacti.

Small signs to say you're there, evidence
Of other people's lives, they warm,
They quicken, they stave off death. They satisfy.

Lyric

Something is happening that never, ever,
Happened to anyone before, he thought.
This is the moment when the sudden river
Breaks through the rocks to flow and end the drought.
Sitting straight-backed upon the bedside chair
She took pins from her lips and fixed her hair.

Give me just this, he thought, let me for ever
Be sitting here with this, without a thought.
Ice ages come, to freeze the flowing river,
Still ponds surround us both, to cool the drought.
Taking each eye in turn, she painted it,
Using a brush, a block of black, and spit.

Frontiers

Even for me, who never goes near one
There is something disturbingly potent
About the notions that go with frontiers.

The movies help, of course, the stage-dressing
Of armed and neutral camps between striped poles
Where tired spies are swapped for tired spies.

And it has something to do with frontiers
That edge-of-town hotels are often known
For goings-on, straight faces and false names.

All that paraphernalia of passports
And men in boots and uniforms! But feeling
That when you pass one you have passed a test

Must come from something older; that you've done
Something vaguely illegal, though licensed,
And satisfied proper authority

That was quite right to stare at you so hard.
But underneath all that, there's more. The sense
That even though frontiers grow usual

There's one remaining. Somewhere in the North,
Most likely, and you'll come to it at night,
Half-way from maps to rumours, on a line

That the ice-bound train won't cross. Reaching it
You'll disembark, ignored by silent guards,
Discard your passport, duck beneath the poles . . .

Seen from the Train

Stopped for a moment. The rain has gone, and
Left behind a light so green and tolerant
The hillside and the houses angled there
Seem more than real. A supernatural
Ordinariness announces that tomorrow
We shall be older, but apart from that,
Nothing important will alter, nothing will move.

All on a level the bottom branches
Of trees in open order in that meadow
Will darken a plane six feet above the green;

In that far corner, porcupined with reeds,
A boggy dip will mark where pathways meet;
And in a silence deep as patience, farms
Unmanned and busy reach across the hills.

My train moves on, and leaves me thinking how
It's most especially when they do not lie
Hardened by snapshot sunlight, these hills and fields,
Into flat tricks of light and shade
But solid in dull air retain their distances,
They move me most. Moving, I make them wheel.

How still they'd be, if I could be so still.

In and Out

Raking a fire, November morning, out in the garden,
Fly from the embers, skirling upwards, black scraps of paper;
Yesterday's news.
Today the news is fog has invaded, year has hardened.

Along the saltings, commas that rise and spatter a vast
Grey nowhere are suddenly birds; seen, they settle,
Beakily, you think,
Embarrassed. Caught disturbing the year's first frost.

Which is, after all, only a warning. Later it will be harder.

But, for the moment, riding past backs of houses,
How comforting to see, saffron in each dark block,
One lighted window.
Reliable men live there, pursuing reliable courses

Which will take them, you can be sure, out from the
                                              unimportant
Secrets of half-awake bedrooms, knickers, dropped socks,
                                              and turning
Away from the light
With luxurious grumbles, wives who've forgotten they met,

Into this now. Before starting, on bikes with boxes
Wingnutted onto carriers, they'll pause and take the perk
Mortgaged days earn:
A moment to rake the roundel of embers, find an astonishing
glow.

It has lasted, against the odds, all the time they slept.

Yesterday's news was bad: today's will be much better.
Left out in the gathering frost, the fire kept in.
It took so little.
Quick, rake it together. Glittering nights are coming

And longer ones, too, that will test banked timbers and quell
Even the cheekiest birds until well past first light.
Simple lessons, then.
Learn to be still, and moving. There you are out, and in.

To One Dead Woman, About Another

You always used to laugh at talk of death
Cocking one damp, delighted, knowing eye
Brimming at me across the oilcloth. *Shocking, really*
To laugh like this, you'd say, *but I don't know,*

I think it's all the fuss they make that curls me up.
Apt at embroidery, I could make you giggle
Anytime, easily, with some lying tale about
Loose lids, tipped hearses, sliding coffins, uproar.

Well now you're dead, John Wakeman's mum, and I
Apologise too late. Not for the laughter, never, but deeply
For failing to see that we flirted in different places
And I with a silly scarecrow; you with a real cold spectre.

Daredevil Dick, gyrating in front of a paper
Bull like a brave torero, I must have been
A bit of a bore at times to you, who worked
Years nearer the real thing's terrain. Were you really laughing?

But now, something of mine died in December.
Shifty in the wind by the raw trench, in a flat
Graveyard with neither grace nor fervour, *Nice,*
We said, *and neat, to have the stones one regulation size.*

That funeral was bitter. Any film director
Would have been rapt to record how her eldest son
Shuddered while she gave birth to winter. (The freezing
Wind that was making his eyes so wet would not have shown.)

Months ago now, that was. Now I can grow sentimental,
Recall her stories. A bull got loose in the farmyard, and,
A girl then, she hid in this big, old-fashioned copper wash
Boiler, you know, in the dairy, pulled the lid over. Zeppelins

Flew overhead into searchlight beams and Grandad
Held her high on his shoulder to see. Like a silver cigar.
At eleven she went to a witch, well, a wise woman really,
In a thick wood outside Whitby, was cured of a squint by
                                                    infusions.

But remember who she was? Not often. Easier, when she
Intrudes, to dredge another of her stories up, a spell
To keep the cold out. Fabulous times, surely she must
Have been so happy then, so long before my time?

And at the grave, remember her? Not then. Regretted, of course,
The pauper's share I gave her, but only mildly. Selfish
As always, my first thought. *She's gone, the barricade*
That stood between me and the rotting earth is down.

And so, dear Mrs Wakeman, this ashamed
Confession that now I grow afraid to die.
Lucky for you, perhaps, that you—come on, let's play
That old game one more time—are dead already,

For if you weren't, you'd surely—wait for it—
Die laughing at this solemn coward who once knew
For certain that he understood you; loved his mother; who
Wishes he still knew that, to charm his fear away.

Transferred Pain

'It's transferred pain,' my jovial dentist said,
Meaning, I think,
The aching peg I'd pointed at was sound,
The trouble altogether elsewhere. How profound!

And 'How profound,' I thought, ten minutes on,
Moling my tongue around my frozen jaw,
To find a lack where I had least expected one.

So deep, so wide a lack, and so surprising. How profound.

Looking South-West

Above and to the south-west, what passes
For a forest; five hundred yards of oak
And beech, well coppiced.

Even that much would seem out of scale, but
For the way the evening sun, behind it,
Makes its soft fringe stiff,

And black and definite. A hard edge to
What would be endless beckoning on a plain,
It's a great comfort.

Not that comfort is hard to come by, in
These fields. Walkers for days, they say, would find
More of much the same.

Not too neat, adapted, still adaptable,
What if they lie? 'Landscape?' they say, 'Landscape, oh, that
Must be shrunk to fit.'

BIOGRAPHICAL NOTES

PETER DIDSBURY: Born 1946, Fleetwood, Lancashire, and moved to Hull at the age of six. He read English and Hebrew at Balliol College, Oxford, and taught English in Hull for eight years until he became redundant. His first collection of poems, *The Butchers of Hull*, has just been published by Bloodaxe Books.

TONY FLYNN: Born 1951, Haslingden, Lancashire. Studied Philosophical Theology at the University of Hull and did research there and at Leicester. He is now a social worker, and lives in Walsall. His pamphlet *Separations* was published in the Proem series in 1976, and in 1980 his first book-length collection *A Strange Routine* appeared from Bloodaxe. He received a Gregory Award in 1977.

IAN GREGSON: Born 1953. Read English at Oxford and researched his Ph.D on H.D. at the University of Hull. He now lectures in English at University College of North Wales, Bangor. He received a Gregory Award in 1981.

T.F. GRIFFIN: Born 1949. Lived in Hull from 1969 to 1975. He has published several pamphlets, and his work has appeared in many magazines. Now lives in Leeds.

DOUGLAS HOUSTON: Born 1947, Cardiff. Studied English at the University of Hull from 1966 to 1969, and then worked in Hull as a schoolteacher. He taught English in Germany before returning to Hull to work on a Ph.D in modern poetry; recently moved to Wales. His first book of poems will appear from Bloodaxe in 1983.

MARGOT K. JUBY: Born 1956. Read English at the University of Hull, took a first in 1977, and has been unemployed in Hull ever since. Her pamphlet *Femme Fatale* (Sol Publications) appeared in 1979.

SEAN O'BRIEN: Born 1952, London, and spent many years in Hull. He read English at Cambridge, Birmingham and Hull; now married and teaches in Sussex. He received a Gregory

Award in 1979. His first collection of poems, *The Indoor Park*, will be published by Bloodaxe Books in autumn 1982.

TONY PETCH: Born 1942. Graduated in Forestry from Edinburgh in 1964, and three years later trained in Edinburgh as a social worker. He is now a training officer with the Social Services Department of Humberside County Council.

GENNY RAHTZ was born during the War in Bristol. She worked on archaeological excavations and did odd jobs before studying Social Administration at the University of Hull and doing research. She now works as a part-time tutor for the Open University.

FRANK REDPATH: Born 1927. Went to school at Hymers College, Hull. He served in the Army from 1944 to 1948, and then worked as a journalist for IPC. He attended the University of Hull from 1965 to 1968, and since 1973 has taught at Hull College of Further Education.